Doing Your Early Years
Research Project

Education at SAGE

SAGE is a leading international publisher of journals, books, and electronic media for academic, educational, and professional markets.

Our education publishing includes:

- accessible and comprehensive texts for aspiring education professionals and practitioners looking to further their careers through continuing professional development

- inspirational advice and guidance for the classroom

- authoritative state of the art reference from the leading authors in the field

Find out more at: **www.sagepub.co.uk/education**

Doing Your Early Years
Research Project

A STEP-BY-STEP GUIDE

2nd Edition

Guy Roberts-Holmes

Los Angeles | London | New Delhi
Singapore | Washington DC

First edition published 2005
Second edition published 2011

SAGE Publications Ltd
1 Oliver's Yard
55 City Road
London EC1Y 1SP

SAGE Publications Inc.
2455 Teller Road
Thousand Oaks, California 91320

SAGE Publications India Pvt Ltd
B 1/I 1 Mohan Cooperative Industrial Area
Mathura Road
New Delhi 110 044

SAGE Publications Asia-Pacific Pte Ltd
33 Pekin Street #02-01
Far East Square
Singapore 048763

Library of Congress Control Number: 2010934514

British Library Cataloguing in Publication data

A catalogue record for this book is available from the British Library

ISBN 978-1-84920-519-1
ISBN 978-1-84920-520-7 (pbk)

Typeset by C&M Digitals (P) Ltd, Chennai, India
Printed in Great Britain by TJ International, Padstow, Cornwall
Printed on paper from sustainable resources

This book is dedicated to my dear brother Paul 'Pablo' Christopher Roberts-Holmes. Paul's love, warmth, humour and passion for life are greatly missed by all who knew him.
August 2nd 1964–February 5th 2001

Contents

About the Author

In the 1980s Guy Roberts-Holmes worked as one of the very few male nursery and reception teachers in Inner London. He thoroughly enjoyed this experience and was eager for more insight into inclusionary/exclusionary professional cultures amongst early years staff, which led to his Master's degree at King's College London. He then worked in The Gambia, West Africa for Voluntary Services Overseas (VSO) as a lecturer at The University of The Gambia. Whilst in The Gambia he was sponsored by The University of Nottingham to carry out an ethnography of a nursery and primary school, leading to the award of his PhD. He taught at Canterbury Christ Church University College and Swansea University. Currently, he is the Programme Leader for the internationally renowned MA Early Years Education at the Institute of Education, University of London. His research interests include research methodologies; gender; digital learning and the professionalisation of the early years workforce.

Acknowledgements

This book has been inspired by my fantastic children, Justin, Pia and Isabelle and their wonderful cousins, Lucinda, Rose, Mary, Oliver, Jane and Tom.

Thank you to the Early Childhood Studies students who shared their research projects with me: Shelley Angel, Lisa Burnap, Gemma Cook, Stephanie Dennehy, Katherine Gough, Martyn Kitney, Eleanor MacDonald, Georgina Moxon and Minsiew Yap.

The author and publisher are grateful for permission to reproduce the following material in this book:

Figure 1.2 from L. Blaxter, C. Hughes and M. Tight (2001), *How to Research*, 2nd edition, Open University Press/McGraw-Hill Publishing Company.

Figure 4.6 from P. Clough and C. Nutbrown (2007), *A Student's Guide to Methodology*, Sage Publications.

Figures 6.2, 6.3 and 6.4 from Y. Lancaster and V. Broadbent (2010), *Listening to Young Children*, Open University Press/McGraw-Hill Publishing Company.

Figure 7.1 from A. Clark and P. Moss (2001), *Listening to Young Children: The Mosaic Approach*, NCB and the Joseph Rowntree Foundation, now updated with the Third Stage of Mosaic; deciding areas of continuity and change in *Spaces to Play*.

English trans. by Lella Gandini © Lella Gandini, 1983. First published in English in *The Hundred Languages of Children: The Reggio Emilia Approach to Early Childhood Education*, 1st edition, edited by Carolyn Edwards, Lella Gandini and George Forman, 1993, and *The Hundred Languages of Children: The Reggio Emilia Approach, Advanced Reflections, 2nd edition*, 1998, Ablex Publishing. © Carolyn Edwards, Lella Gandini and George Forman, 1993, 1998. Reproduced with permission of Greenwood Publishing Group, Inc., Westport, CT.

Edwards, C., Gandini, L. and Forman, G. *The Hundred Languages of Children: The Reggio Emilia Approach to Early Childhood Education*. From the Catalogue of the Exhibition 'The Hundred Languages of Children', © Preschools and Infant-toddler Centers – Instituzione of the Municipality of Reggio Emilia, Italy, published by Reggio Children, 1996.

Reggio Children/Centro Internazionale Loris Malaguzzi, Via Bligny, 1/a
42124 Reggio Emilia, http://zerosei.comune.re.it/

Foreword

It is a great pleasure to write the foreword to the second edition of *Doing Your Early Years Research Project*. Since it was first published in 2005 Guy Roberts-Holmes' original book has always been extremely well received by the early childhood and children and family studies students that I teach on both undergraduate and postgraduate courses, including many of whom are practitioners and a number of children's centre leaders who are engaging in their first recognised research project. The students comment that they like the clear style, helpful and 'step by step' guidance and also recognise the ethical, reflective and rigorous approach to research with children, families and practitioners that the book fosters.

The welcome publication of this second edition comes at a challenging time for those working in early childhood education and care in England due to the severe financial cut backs and re-organisation imposed by a newly elected government in May 2010. Whilst, at the time of writing, the fine detail of these changes is still to be finalised, it is clear that research in the field by both practitioners and students will become ever more vital to understand, explain and critique the changing landscape of children's services and children's lives. At the same time, although children's need for 'warm human relationships, real and active experience, security and play with other children' may not have changed since Susan Isaacs (1954: 3) work was published nearly sixty years ago, new approaches from sociology, cross-cultural perspectives and post-modern views have challenged traditional discourses (Yelland, Lee, O'Rourke and Hanlon, 2008) and influenced our professional work, understanding of childhoods and significantly the way we research children's lives. Much research is now focused on research *with* children, drawing on children's perspectives rather than just the adult's opinions of the way children live their lives. Thus reflecting the values, beliefs and assumptions many early childhood practitioners and researchers hold in relation to children, including their competence, rights and role within the research (Harcourt, Perry and Waller, 2011 *forthcoming*). *Doing Your Early Years Research Project* reflects this recent development (Kellett, 2010) and guides students towards the successful completion of their project.

One of the real strengths of this book is how students are gently but ethically and persuasively encouraged to engage in reflective research and supported throughout their project with clear structured guidance and examples from real research projects. At the outset of their research many students are apprehensive and Roberts-Holmes sensitively pilots readers through some of the possible initial anxieties and challenges, focusing on the importance of critical reflection and reflective practice research as part of professional practice in the early years.

This second edition has been updated and enhanced by further consideration of the importance of the underlying theory (methodology) behind the research project and how this methodology determines the design and methods used to gather and analyse data. Here, there is an expanded discussion of research design and sampling approach. Many students new to research find the development of focused research questions problematic and this book offers clear guidance on developing appropriate questions for investigation, with the use of helpful diagrams. Further aspects of the research process such as data reduction, coding and analysing findings are carefully unpicked. Increasingly software such as NVivo is being used to assist data reduction in qualitative research and this edition includes a valuable section introducing readers to using computer software to assist in the organisation, analysis and display of data.

Through reading and using this book students and practitioner researchers, undertaking a range of early childhood and children and family studies related degrees, are well placed to undertake successful investigations and to help evolve the debate and understanding of young children's lives and professional work in early childhood.

Tim Waller
Reader in Early Years Education
University of Wolverhampton

Glossary

Action research   Action research or practitioner research attempts to instigate change in the form of improved practice, policy and culture within an institution. Action research is a collaborative and participatory research approach.

Article 12   Article 12 of the United Nations *Convention on the Rights of the Child* (UN, 1989) declares that children have the right to hold an opinion about issues concerning them. Article 12 encourages early childhood researchers to engage children in research that affects them and to listen and act upon what children say.

Case study   Case studies are useful for finding out more about the detailed, subtle and complex social interactions and processes operating within a narrowly defined context such as a single early childhood centre or family.

Child-centred methodology   The ethical values and principles which place children centre stage throughout the research process, for example, the Mosaic approach.

Documentation   A range of evidence collected by and with young children about their early childhood institution. Documentation in the form of children's, practitioners' and parents' photographs, drawings, consultations and observations can be built up to provide a mosaic of perspectives on the early childhood institution.

Ethics   Ethical research involves respect and sensitivity to the feelings and rights of *all* those participating in your research project. Ethical researchers carefully reflect upon any unintended harm that they may cause to the participants.

Ethnography   Early childhood ethnographies aim to provide holistic accounts of the views, perspectives, beliefs and values of the children, practitioners, workers and parents in an early childhood institution.

Focus group conversations   A collaborative interview technique particularly effective with young children. Children may be empowered in a focus group in which they feel comfortable.

Gatekeepers   Gatekeepers decide whether or not you can proceed with your research in the institution they manage. Headteachers, early childhood centre managers and children's supervisors can all act as gatekeepers.

Informed consent Informed consent refers to the ethical principle of research participants voluntarily agreeing to participate in a research project based upon complete disclosure of all relevant information and the recipient's understanding of this. Early childhood researchers are expected to gain informed consent from all the research participants in their study. Issues of informed consent with young children hinge on whether the children competently understand what is expected of them in the research process.

Interpretivism Interpretivists believe that the social world is continually being created and constructed. Shared understandings and meanings are given to these social interactions.

Interviews Interviews are on a continuum from the closed structured interview to the unstructured consultation. In order to listen respectfully to young children, early childhood researchers focus upon child-centred participatory activities such as children's drawings during the consultation.

Interview guide A set of predetermined field questions which direct the flow of the interview.

Methodology Methodology refers to the principles and values, philosophies and ideologies that underpin the entire research process. Your methodology will inform the questions that you ask, the literature you read, your methods and the analysis. Early childhood studies research is frequently driven by a child-centred methodology in which the child comes first.

Methods Methods are the actual techniques that the researcher uses to answer their field questions. Examples of methods include case studies, questionnaires, interviews and observation.

Objectivity Historically, researchers mistakenly believed in a neutral and disengaged researcher whose beliefs, politics and experiences did not affect the research in any way. In early childhood studies, as in other social sciences, researcher objectivity has been seen as a myth and a fallacy. Hence the need for reflexivity throughout the research process.

Observation schedule An observational checklist on which specific observations concerning a targeted child or children are made.

Participant observation The researcher takes part in the activities with the participants and at the same time reflects upon and researches the situation.

Pilot study A pilot study involves the researcher trialling the interview questions, the questionnaires, the observations and any forms of research methods.

The pilot study can alert the researcher to any potential future difficulties and the research can be appropriately amended.

Positivism Positivists believe that the social world of people operates in a similar way to the natural physical world. Thus notions of researcher subjectivity and reflexivity are not issues within the positivist tradition. The positivist tradition attempts to prove hypotheses.

Probing An interview research technique for eliciting information from the respondent.

Qualitative methods Qualitative research methods usually involve non-numerical data collection, such as interviews, participant observation, diaries, drawings and children's photographs. Qualitative research tends to produce and analyse in-depth and detailed data. Qualitative research methods may be combined with quantitative research methods.

Quantitative methods Quantitative research methods usually involve numerical data collection derived from questionnaires, statistical surveys and experiments. Quantitative research tends to produce and analyse broad contextual data providing overall patterns and generalisations. Quantitative research methods may be combined with qualitative research methods.

Research diary Your research diary is a reflective log of your thoughts and feelings as they occur during the research process. Extracts from your reflective research diary may be used in your research study when triangulated with additional pieces of data confirming your thoughts and feelings.

Research participants Includes all those who work with and provide material for the research project, for example, colleagues, children, workers, teachers, practitioners and parents.

Reflexivity Reflexive researchers are self-aware of their biases, assumptions and interpretations of the research issues. Self-awareness of how the researcher affects the children and adults constantly informs reflexive research. Practitioner-researchers need to demonstrate self-awareness and sensitivity to the ways in which their presence affects the data they collect and how their underlying assumptions make them interpret the data in particular ways.

Sampling is the way in which a researcher chooses the setting(s), practitioner(s), child(ren) that they actually study. Quantitative researchers tend to randomly sample as they are attempting to make their research representative. Qualitative researchers tend to use purposive sampling to explain or understand the phenomena that they are studying. They also may often use convenience sampling.

Structured observations Focused and targeted observations such as specific child observations, event sampling and targeted running records.

Subjectivity A researcher's subjectivity refers to the extent that the researcher's own feelings, biases and interpretations influence the research questions, data collection and interpretation. Hence subjectivity is closely connected to reflexivity. Researcher subjectivity is sometimes used to critique researcher objectivity.

Survey Surveys attempt to produce large volumes of broad and generalisable data using questionnaires with a large sample size. Surveys use a variety of sampling methods.

Social justice Social justice research aims to make a positive contribution to the broader social good for *all* young children, their families and communities. Social justice is at the heart of politically transformative research. Fairness, justice, equality and respect are some of the principles and values underpinning social justice research.

Triangulation Triangulation involves the comparison and combination of different sources of evidence in order to reach a better understanding of the research topic. Thus the researcher's observations, interviews with participants and questionnaires all produce different pieces of evidence which can be combined and compared to give a triangulated analysis.

Unstructured observations Typically these are in the form of reflective diary notes and anecdotal unfocused observations on the early childhood setting. When combined with triangulated evidence from practitioners, workers and parents, they can be included as data in the research report.

Validity The interpretivist and positivist research traditions have different understandings of research validity. For the interpretivist, triangulation of participants' responses is used so that the participants' true voices are seen to be consistent and valid. For the positivist, validity is concerned with the research process and findings being replicated or copied by another researcher.

1

You can do research!

Learning objectives

This chapter will help you to:

- understand and demystify the process of research
- express your feelings about carrying out a research project
- understand the importance of social justice in research
- appreciate the importance of reflective practice in research
- understand the principles of high-quality research
- appreciate the everyday research skills which you already possess
- understand your supervisor's and your responsibilities for the project.

Your feelings about doing research

As you start your research project you are probably feeling a whole range of emotions. The following sections cover a wide variety of emotions that some students stated they felt about their forthcoming early childhood research projects. The students' positive feelings are concerned with the excitement of focusing in depth upon an issue which is of real interest to them and working at their own pace and helping children. The anxieties the students have include being apprehensive about their own abilities and not having sufficient time. These positive and negative feelings about research topics are extremely common. Your early apprehension will help you to generate the enthusiasm to successfully complete your research project.

As you read through the students' comments below think about the following questions:

- Which comments do you empathise with?

- Why do you think so many students feel this way?

- How do you feel at the moment about doing your research project? Talk your feelings through with your friends and with your supervisor.

I'm looking forward to …

- The idea of 'digging deep' into an area that really interests me is a real energy booster.

- I'm very excited about my project as it is a topic which I'm fascinated about.

- The idea of doing research gives me 'a buzz'. It's a great opportunity to learn, to evaluate and to evolve ideas.

- I feel that this is a good opportunity to gain further insight into an area of early childhood studies which really interests ME.

- We can choose exactly what we want to look at and I can work at my own pace.

- I want to make a change for the better and help children through my research.

Anxieties

- I hope I can go into sufficient depth in the area in the short time-span and do the topic the justice it deserves.

- I'm worried about not being able to get enough material together and not having the time to complete the study.

- As a single mum with three children the amount of time I will have to spend on the project concerns me. Will I have enough time?

- It feels like an enormous undertaking because I'm just not sure what I will be researching!

- I'm anxious about being out of my depth!

- I am wondering whether I am confident enough to ask professionals the questions I need answering.

- I feel I need a lot of guidance and support and hope this will be available to me.

- I am a bit wary about how to approach my area, however, once I start talking to lecturers and people in the setting I feel that most of these apprehensions will disappear.

- I worry about the ethical issues.

- Am I organised enough to carry out such a project?

Myths about early childhood research

The above range of feelings may arise because the very word 'research' can for some create anxiety. It is important to remember that research is simply a tool, (MacNaughton et al., 2010). Like any other tool, when you learn what it does, why it has been invented and how to use it, it becomes beneficial to you. This means that, because research is just a tool, you are in control of it, rather than it being in control of you. The negative associations that you may be feeling about the word 'research' are not unusual and can stem from commonly held myths and stereotypes. The following wrong and mistaken views about research do sometimes create emotional barriers which prevent early childhood practitioners from participating in the research process.

- Early childhood research can only be done by academic professors and experts.

- The research process is so intellectual, complex, mysterious and time-consuming that it cannot possibly be for people like me!

- Research produces hard facts which are unquestionable.

- Research proves things one way or the other.
- There is only one way to do research.
- Research is a strict scientific exercise.
- Research is boring.
- Research cannot change anything.
- There are not any real benefits from doing research. (Adapted from Blaxter et al., 2010.)

An inclusive approach towards early childhood research

Below are listed some different and more inclusive viewpoints about research which many early childhood practitioners have found to be true for them.

- You already possess many 'everyday' research skills.
- Research can be done by everybody – this means you too!
- Research is simply a tool for you to use.
- Research is fun and hard work.
- Research asks questions about things that really matter to us.
- Research can initiate personal and professional change and development.
- Research is about developing knowledge.
- Research is about discovery.
- Research is about change.
- Research helps us to understand complex issues in childhood.
- Research helps to further professionalise early childhood studies.
- Research is about questioning taken for granted assumptions, myths and 'commonsense' understandings.
- Research is about challenging habitual patterns of behaviour.
- Research can satisfy your fascination with an issue.
- Research can positively benefit you, your work, the children and the setting you work in.

Which of the above statements do you agree and disagree with? To what extent do you agree with the following statement?

- Early childhood research enables us to see things about children and ourselves as practitioners in new and different ways, to challenge our habitual patterns of thinking and to possibly act in new ways.

You might be wondering what you can offer to early childhood research. The good news is that early childhood is a rapidly expanding area and you can contribute to that process with your research project.

Your research project within early childhood studies

Although a lot has been written about early childhood and children, there is still a great deal that is unknown concerning young children growing up in society. Today's complex society increasingly places responsibilities upon early childhood practitioners to understand more about children. New legislation, policies and practice constantly change the ways in which practitioners must relate and work with the child(ren) in their care. For example, within the UK the Early Years Foundation Stage (DCSF, 2008) poses huge challenges for early years practitioners in implementing its laudable principles and aims. The EYFS has increased expectations of early childhood services and the people who work in them. There is a tremendous need to know more about the different ways in which these changing complex factors influence children and their childhoods.

Childhoods are understood as being positioned within a set of overlapping complex issues (Bronfenbrenner, 1979; Rogoff, 2003). Childhoods are not experienced within a vacuum but, rather, connected to a whole range of sociological issues such as class, ethnicity, gender and geographical location. Within society children are holistically influenced by the type of early childhood setting they go to, their schools, their health care and the media. All these issues impact upon different children in different ways. In these complex ways childhoods are understood in a holistic way. This knowledge of the complexity of childhood leads us to ask many questions about children. This is where the research tool can help us to begin to answer some of those questions. So, as an early childhood practitioner you can begin to see why you must be engaged in research; there is so much more to learn about children and their varied childhoods!

The professionalisation of early childhood studies

It is important to note that research is a powerful tool in developing early childhood professionalism (MacNaughton et al., 2010). So whatever your motivations in coming to this book, whether to develop critical skills in reading about research done by others, or because you wish to carry out research for yourself, you will be helping with the ongoing professionalisation of early childhood studies.

You might want to know more about early childhood research for a variety of reasons. It might be a compulsory project as part of your course assessment. You might be a practitioner working with children in some capacity and you wish to carry out a small-scale study as part of your work with the intention of improving your practice in your institution. Such practitioner action research is increasingly important in developing and improving early childhood practice. This book will help you to ask research-style questions about your own current practice, the collection of evidence, its analysis, and any possible conclusions that can be drawn. Early childhood practitioners are therefore increasingly recognised as important participants in the culture of childhood research.

By reading this book you will inform yourself about what constitutes high-quality, valid research. This will make you a better 'consumer' of research and policy. By understanding the process of high-quality research based upon ethical values and principles, you will be able to review and reflect upon the research you read with more confidence and more effectively. By being aware of what constitutes high-quality ethical research you will be able to critically evaluate research conducted by others. Such critical reflection upon research carried out by others is central to the process of professionalism within early childhood studies.

By aspiring to be an 'evidence-based profession' early childhood practitioners move beyond mere response to whatever the next government policy or initiative might be to a more powerful and informed position. Much early childhood practice is currently led by government policy. By becoming informed consumers of research and actually carrying out research yourself, you can generate your own knowledge and understanding. Such understanding is useful in the process of responding to policy initiatives. For example, by having read research evidence on emotional literacy in the early years and perhaps carrying out research on emotional literacy with children you are in a better position to review government policies which address, or omit, emotional development in young children.

The importance of your reflective practice

Some early childhood practitioners incorrectly create a division in their own minds between an imagined 'academic high ground' and the 'swampy lowlands' (Schön, 1987). They feel that 'thinking about practice' (which is what reflective practice is) belongs to an 'academic high ground' which is not for them. These practitioners wrongly feel that they should just *do* practice and not *think about* practice. This is because they incorrectly believe that the 'practice' of doing early childhood research and 'thinking about it' are disconnected and separate. Such attitudes can act as a self-limiting barrier to one's potential. Practitioners who engage in reflective practice can produce real-world knowledge grounded within their work. By engaging in a process of reflective practice, practitioners can create real-world knowledge born from experience and critical reflection. Reflection involves thinking about a particular aspect of your work and how to improve it. This process of reflection is personal but it may also be done with your trusted critical friends and or colleagues.

Reflective practice is about improving practice and generating theories to understand that improvement. Such real-world knowledge produced by early childhood practitioners is as good as that within the 'established' academic community. In order to ensure that your real-world knowledge has validity you must demonstrate that it involves critical reflection and a systematic enquiry. The key message is that early years professionals can and do produce original thinking. This is because although people may well have carried out research into your topic area before, nobody has ever done your particular piece of research in your particular setting before. Schön (1987) made a distinction between 'reflection in action' and 'reflection on action'. Reflection in action is about 'thinking on your feet', which is what early years practitioners do all the time of course! Reflection on action is a more subtle and mature retrospective thinking or 'thinking after the event'. Early years professional reflective practice primarily involves thinking after the event about what happened and *why*.

Your reflective practice research in your unique early years context may throw up original insights and thoughts about the topic area. '[I]f you are not heard, you will continue to be marginalized and not ... be taken seriously' ... (McNiff, 2006: 49). Through engaging in a systematic process of reflective practice research it is possible that your 'voice' can be heard in the field of early childhood.

With reflective practice *you* take control of *your* situation. You are the script writer, the stage director and the main actor/actress. Yes it is your play! You own the research and it is personal and meaningful to you. This is why reflective practice is so empowering. You become the insider researcher with the passion and enthusiasm to make insightful observations and improvements in your early years setting. You become the expert doer and thinker. You can generate your theories as to what worked and why and perhaps learn from what changes didn't work and why. McNiff (2006) has noted that reflective practice generates *sustainable* change because the practitioner is central. The practitioner creates and implements their own ideas rather than the ideas of an outside expert.

What does reflective practice involve?

Reflective practice is concerned with you investigating and evaluating your early years work. Reflective practice is concerned with you taking action to improve your personal, social and professional early years context. The main questions that early years reflective practitioners ask are based upon the following:

- What am I doing?
- Why am I doing it this way?
- How can I improve upon what I am doing?

These questions are at the heart of any early years reflective practice research project. From these practical projects it is possible for early years practitioners to generate their own personal theories about what works in an early years setting and what doesn't work. Hence reflective practice is concerned with *both* the practical aspects of doing your job better *and* generating knowledge about why you believe your practice has improved.

Below are some questions which highlight the differences between outsider type questions (traditional research) and insider type questions (action research).

Traditional research questions	Reflective practice research questions
What is the relationship between children and the outdoor environment?	How can I improve the use of the outdoor area?
What is the connection between management style and increased motivation?	How can I improve my working relationships with my support staff?

Why do early years policy documents generally not include young children's thinking?	How can I listen more carefully to young children's ideas about what they think they should be learning?
What is the relationship between enhanced family involvement and children's learning?	How can I get families more involved in my early years setting?

In the above questions you can see that you, the practitioner, are centrally involved in the research process. 'I' is used in all the reflective practice research questions because you the practitioner are central and you are asking questions about your professional work. You know your setting and yourself and as a well trained reflective practitioner you know the sorts of questions you need to ask to improve your practice. Reflective practice thus presents a fundamentally different approach to traditional research. Within reflective practice you are much more powerfully positioned since you are in control of the process from start to finish.

Reflective practice research as professional development

Reflective practice is centrally concerned with your process of professional development, change and improvement. Practitioner research is an integral part of your critical professional development (Schon, 1987). As a professional you constantly need to reflect upon work and ways in which to enhance your work with young children. The underlying principles and values of reflective practice should be integral to everything you do in your work.

As a professional you constantly need to reflect upon your work. Increasingly early years professionals need to be accountable. For example, within the Early Years Professional Status (EYPS) the required Standard S38 explicitly states that candidates for EYPS are to 'Reflect on and evaluate the impact of practice' (CWDC, 2010: 88). To be accountable you need to be able to justify what you are doing and why you are doing it. Your reflective practice project will help you to understand an issue in much more depth. This understanding will help you to justify your professional actions. The following is a summary of some of the ways in which reflective practice research can help you develop your early years professionalism.

1. A deeper understanding of your values and principles
Reflection involves thinking about a particular aspect of your work and how to improve it. This process of reflection is personal and it may also be done

with your trusted critical friends or colleagues. Informed and insightful reflection is a central aspect of personal and professional development. This will lead to an enhanced understanding of your professional values and principles.

2. Increased professionalism

Through engaging in the process of reflective practice you will develop your interests and motivation in your work leading to further reflection and development. A positive cycle of personal and professional development can develop from your initial small-scale project.

3. Enhanced working relationships with children, parents and colleagues

Reflective practice is very often a collaborative venture and can involve close working with colleagues, children, families and communities. Reflective practice can be a sociable experience carried out with trusted colleagues or critical friends.

4. Developing your pedagogic skills and knowledge

Critical reflection can arise out of your desire to enhance your teaching skills and knowledge of how you can help children best develop emotionally, cognitively, physically and spiritually. Much practice with young children involves holistic learning. Reflective practice can be sensitive to the subtle and complex learning processes of young children.

5. Increased theoretical knowledge and engagement

One of the great benefits of engaging in reflective practice is that it is your project and you may wish to develop not only your practical knowledge but also your theoretical knowledge of the issues. You read other people's ideas about the early years issues and together with your experience and insight you can generate your own knowledge and understanding about what works and why. In this way reflective practice is empowering and can give meaning to practitioners' working lives. Early years workers engaged in reflective practice develop personal 'living theories' (Whitehead, 2006) about themselves and their work. As you share these 'living theories' increasingly you become more confident in your own thinking and theories about your practice. This increased confidence and awareness of *why* you do *what* you do is part of your professionalisation process.

6. Developed self respect, power and self-esteem
Early years workers who engage in reflective practice projects feel more powerful. This is because action research is about you taking the lead responsibility for developing your personal and professional work. This can lead to an increased sense of empowerment and enjoyment from your work. Action research can thus initiate positive cycles of personal and professional development. A worthwhile piece of action research that you personally believe in can empower and transform your working life. You will feel more powerful in your work as you come to reflect and change it in various ways for the better.

7. Increased respect for children
Some reflective practice projects involve listening to children's perceptions and understandings. Such projects can highlight what you already know; that young children are strong and have immense abilities and competencies if we allow them. It is we adults who need to listen and see children better.

8. Increased awareness of the wider contexts in which you work
Much of your work as an early years professional is framed by various pieces of government legislation and policy guidance such as the Early Years Foundation Stage (DCSF, 2008). As you engage in your research project your awareness will be raised of the wider policy contexts in which you, your work and your early years setting are situated. This increased awareness and knowledge may lead you to further action research projects.

9. Increased confidence with research skills
By carrying through a piece of reflective practice research you will gain experience and knowledge of how to successfully plan and engage a research project. This will develop your confidence in this important aspect of your professional development. You will be able to answer people who cite research and evidence with your own knowledge and understanding to justify what you are doing and why. This is a powerful and professional way of engagement.

Principles of high-quality early childhood research

Regardless of the topic of your research project there are some basic principles which underpin all quality early childhood research. The underpinning values and principles of high-quality research can be summarised as follows (MacNaughton et al., 2010).

Your research should be:

- critical and political
- ethical
- respectful of children's participatory rights
- purposeful
- well designed
- transparent
- honest about your assumptions.

The critical research stance

Critical researchers would argue that at the heart of their research is a desire to *transform and change* people (Clough and Nutbrown, 2007). For the purposes of a small-scale project this transformation is often about the researcher themselves developing their understanding through enhanced knowledge and experience by actually doing the research. Ultimately, critical research is concerned with the transformation of people, their institutions and, thus, society itself.

Social justice is at the heart of any critical research. The principles underpinning critical research include fairness, justice, equality and respect. Chapter 2 describes some personal research stories in which all the researchers had issues of social justice they wished to write about. Such social justice issues included race equality, patriarchy and the violent oppression of women and children, unfair gender stereotypes, and a desire to listen to children's perspectives in the schooling process.

The point is to keep a critical stance throughout the research process. To do this the researcher must continuously ask questions about their assumptions and underlying beliefs. The researcher needs to be aware of power issues in their topic. Issues of racism, sexism, classism, violence and the negation of children's rights do not occur in a political vacuum. Within critical research the interactions and structures which allow such abuses of power and inequalities need to be understood, discussed and challenged in your written work.

Critical research involves the researcher being continuously open to alternative views and perspectives. Being critical can include being sceptical of the use of certain everyday terms. For example, critical researchers challenge the thinking that goes along with the label of special educational needs, preferring instead to work with the ideology of inclusion (Booth and Ainscow, 2004).

 Activity

What is it that you would like your research to change and to make better?
What underlying principles of social justice are embedded in your research project?
What power issues are involved in your research?
What everyday terms and thinking about your topic area do you think need changing?

Ethics are central

Ethical issues must be central to any piece of early childhood research. Ethical issues should continuously permeate all aspects of the research process, from the questions or hypotheses asked to the choice of research techniques, and to how the research is presented and fed back to the respondents. All research can potentially be both beneficial and, sometimes, inadvertently harmful. Your research should aim to make a positive contribution to the broader social good within early childhood. Think about the ways in which your project may be beneficial to the children, the setting and to you. You also have to try to predict any possible ill effects your research topic and your questions might have. It is therefore crucial at the outset of any research to think through any possible ethical difficulties, problems and concerns that may arise as a result of your research. Think of these possible difficulties in relation to the children, the setting and you. If you are doing your research as part of a college course, ethical issues might determine whether it is possible to carry out the research or not. So carefully think through any potential ethical difficulties now to avoid disappointment later on. Chapter 4 focuses upon the ethical issues needed in your research.

Children's participatory rights

Increasingly, children themselves are being seen as important people within the research process (http://childrens-research-centre.open.ac.uk). Notions of children's participatory rights in issues which affect them are influencing the ways in which research is carried out. Within the research process, listening to children, consulting with children and respecting children's views are becoming widespread in childhood research. Children actively wish to participate in the research process, for example in the planning for children's services (Kirby et al., 2003). This process of actively engaging with children demands sensitivity from the researcher. The ethical considerations in participatory research with children are changing the ways in which research itself is understood.

Purposeful research

Your research should have clear aims and be worthwhile. The research topic and what it sets out to do should matter to you and to others. If your research is worthwhile it is likely to be interesting and enjoyable – essential if you are to complete your project! Purposeful, clear aims to the research are also crucial in encouraging others to take part in your research.

Your research should be well designed

You should have carefully thought through your research approaches and techniques. How to do this is fully discussed in Chapter 3. Sufficient reading and knowledge will help to inform your research questions or predictive hypotheses, which should also be well thought through. The research should be well organised and achievable within a particular timescale.

Your research should be transparent

Transparent research allows other people to follow your complete research trail. Hence your research should be clear and honest. When other people read your research they should clearly understand what you did and why you did it. Transparency involves letting people know why you took certain decisions in the research process. Transparency is also important for issues of validity.

Developing reflexivity

Perhaps you have chosen your research topic because you have a passionate personal interest in the area and hold a particular viewpoint which you wish to prove. Hence, throughout the research you might be on one side of an argument. Being self-aware of such passionate beliefs, biases and assumptions is known as reflexivity. It is important for researchers to reflect and be self-aware of their own points of view and biases that they bring to the research topic. Such biases or assumptions may inadvertently prevent the researcher from being open to the possibility of different perspectives and understandings of the topic. However, for the purposes of research it is important that you are honest and transparent about your biases and assumptions. Throughout the research process you need continuously to reflect upon how your assumptions and biases might influence your project. This process of self-reflection upon how you might be influencing your research is not always easy to achieve. What assumptions are you making about the topic? You should note down the ways in which you feel biased in the area of your research.

Some early childhood research topics are highly contentious, for example, single parenting, stepfamilies, bullying, gender discrimination, etc. It is hard to remain objective and distant and open to alternative possibilities and viewpoints with such topics. For example, you might choose to look at the issue of bullying within your setting. This emotionally difficult topic might include bullying amongst the children and amongst the staff. You might have chosen this topic because you feel bullied at your workplace. Hence, you might harbour anger and frustration towards your setting. Perhaps, however, for the children and other staff at your setting the anti-bullying policy and practices are effective at preventing and dealing with bullying. Within your setting you must find a range of opinions concerning bullying. Quite possibly some of these other opinions amongst staff, parents and children will support your experiences whilst others may contradict your experiences. The point is to try to remain open to others' viewpoints and perspectives and to reflect upon your own biases and assumptions.

Activity

Think about the assumptions that you hold regarding your research topic.
Write down any strongly held beliefs you have about your topic.
Why do you think you hold these beliefs about your topic?

Activity

Carefully read the papers/magazines for a week and collect examples of research that affects children and families and early childhood. Then answer these questions about the articles:

(Continued)

(Continued)

What do you think of this research?
Does it tell us anything significantly new?
Was it, in your opinion, worth researching and publishing?
Who might benefit from the research?
Does it fulfil the principles for high-quality research?

The research process within early childhood studies

Research within early childhood can be approached in many different ways. Different overall approaches include perceiving research as a linear process or as a recursive spiral process.

In the linear model of early childhood research (Figure 1.1) it is envisaged that there is a set of more or less fixed stages through which the research must pass in orderly fashion.

The straightforward stages in Figure 1.1 provide a useful and needed structure for your research. However, such a fixed model can prove to be rather limiting and constraining.

Stage one
Choosing an early childhood topic

Stage two
Thinking about possible methods

Stage three
Reading about the early childhood topic

Stage four
Collecting the evidence

Stage five
Analysing the evidence

Stage six
Writing up

Figure 1.1 The linear research model

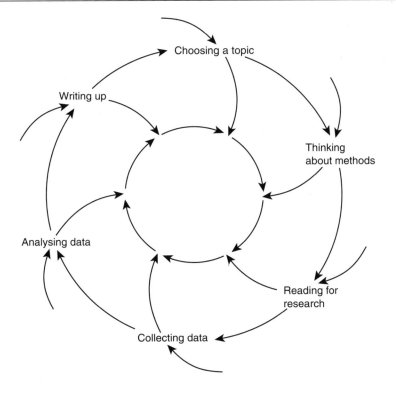

Figure 1.2   The research spiral

Figure 1.2 illustrates the research spiral (Blaxter et al., 2010).

The recursive research spiral is not a fixed process. It allows for the research to be more flexible and open to changes in direction. In this book you are encouraged to revisit any of the research stages in the light of your ongoing understanding, reading and evidence. In the spiral model, research becomes dynamic, fluid and open to change as you progress with your topic. For example, sometimes early childhood researchers can only select their topics after they have read some literature in the area they are interested in. Indeed, reading permeates all stages of the research process. At other times a piece of evidence may emerge in the form of a child's drawing, or what a child says, or a new initiative in your workforce which might lead you to reading and asking different and amended research questions. In these ways the spiral research model is useful because it can be entered at almost any point.

Everyday research skills

To get on your course or be employed within your work setting means that you are already experienced in many everyday research skills – whether you know it or not (Blaxter et al., 2010). However, you are probably unaware of how many research techniques you are already familiar with. Everyday research skills and techniques that you are experienced with include:

- reading

- asking questions

- watching

- listening

- selecting and sorting information

- organising

- writing

- reflecting.

You will probably be very good at some of the above everyday research skills but might never have considered such an ability to be a research skill! For example, to go on a holiday with your friends involves using many of the above everyday research skills. Finding out where to go involves selecting and reading appropriate magazines, websites and books. You may ask friends and family for advice. You have to reflect upon the reading and your friends' advice to make a selection of where and when you go on holiday. You might decide to go to a travel agent. You have to ask a specific set of questions which might include destinations, costs, carriers, travel arrangements for small children, elderly people, etc. You might have to think about appropriate clothes, language and money. You will accumulate a vast amount of material on destinations and travel which needs sorting and organising. You then have to make a selection based upon your information. All the above involves a huge amount of planning, organisation and effort. This book will make these implicit everyday research skills, that you already possess, explicit for you. All these natural skills and abilities that you already possess in order successfully to have a holiday mean that you *can* successfully carry out a small research project. Table 1.1 clearly shows the connections between your everyday life skills and research skills.

Table 1.1 The connections between everyday life skills and their more formal research equivalent

Everyday life skills	Research equivalent
Reading	Reading for research; literature review; documentary analysis
Listening	Interviewing
Watching	Observations
Choosing	Sampling and selection of respondents
Summarising situations, events, television shows, films, etc.	Managing your data
Organising events and situations within a given time frame	Managing your project
Writing	Writing up your project
Reflecting upon life's events and situations	Researcher bias

 ## Activity

Think of an 'everyday' situation that involves using research skills that you already possess, for example, buying a new stereo, choosing your child's child-minder, organising a wedding, buying a car, etc. List what you have to do and the everyday research skills you employ to successfully carry out the task.

Summary

The principles and values underpinning high-quality early childhood research are crucial in producing critical social research that empowers prac-titioners, their institutions and the children in their care. This chapter has begun to demystify the process of research by making explicit the everyday research skills that you already possess. Early childhood studies is an area of rapid growth within society. As integrated and holistic children's services are developed throughout society, so early childhood practitioners' responsi-bilities are increased. Enhanced knowledge about children's complex and varied lives will help to meet these professional responsibilities. Your small-scale research project is an important part of this professionalisation process.

(Continued)

(Continued)

In this chapter you have:

- developed your confidence to 'have a go' at research
- understood the importance of your early childhood studies research project
- appreciated the significance of reflective practice in your research
- examined the principles underpinning high quality early childhood research
- appreciated that research is a process and not a one-off right or wrong event.

Recommended reading 📖

Blaxter, L., Hughes, C. and Tight, M. (2010) *How to Research*, 3rd edn. Buckingham: Open University Press.
This book is an extremely useful how-to guide for early researchers. Chapters 1 and 2 provide an overview of the generic research process. It includes a series of activities for novice practitioners to carry out.

MacNaughton, G., Rolfe, S. and Siraj-Blatchford, I. (eds) (2010) *Doing Early Childhood Research: International Perspectives on Theory and Practice*, 2nd edn. Buckingham: Open University Press.
The second edition of this classic textbook is an excellent guide for both novice and experienced early childhood researchers. The first two chapters provide novice researchers with an in-depth and thorough discussion of the process of early childhood research and the principles of high quality early childhood research.

http://childrens-research-centre.open.ac.uk

This website contains an inspiring collection of 7- and 8-year-old-child-led research projects and resources for including children within the research process. The site contains PowerPoint presentations made by the children themselves and their reflections on the research process.

2

Your research story, methodology and research questions

Reflecting upon your personal story

The aim of this chapter is to help you think of an appropriate early years research topic. The topic needs to be appropriate for you personally *and* professionally. You should try to choose an early childhood research issue which is deeply stimulating to you personally – the heart aspect – and at the same time is of practical professional use for your future career – the head aspect. You need to think both passionately with your heart and strategically with your head. Choosing the right topic at the start is important because it is hard to change halfway through.

This is your research, so the motivations for doing it need to be selfish. You need to own and take responsibility for your research project to complete it successfully. To begin with you need to think of a topic in which you ideally have a deep personal and passionate interest. Such personal enthusiasm will lead to the high levels of motivation needed to sustain your interest throughout the research process.

People choose their research topics for a variety of interrelated personal and professional reasons. Some research topics stem from our personal lives. For example, you may have experienced a significant incident in your life which might lead you to ask further questions about that incident. Sometimes such critical incidents may have occurred with your family, or perhaps at work, and we wish to find out more about the particular issue. Research is sometimes about our own storied lives and making sense of ourselves. Hence when choosing a topic to research it is good to look deep within ourselves to find a topic in which we have a personal interest. This may involve reflection upon our own lives and perhaps critical incidents that have occurred in our lives. Such personal reflection and introspection are not always easy and indeed may prove to be emotionally problematic. You should not be afraid of this since such reflection might well lead you to locate a personally significant and important research topic.

Methodology

Methodology refers to the principles and values, philosophies and ideologies that underpin your research (Clough and Nutbrown, 2007). The methodology that you hold structures how you perceive and understand your research topic and the knowledge that you construct. You may have a variety of values and principles, thus your research may have several methodologies. For example, you could have a child-centred methodology, a feminist methodology and an anti-racist methodology together underpinning your research. These deeply held principles and values which drive your desire to carry out a piece of research form the basis of your research methodology. Reflecting upon your research story will help you to be more aware of your methodology. If the reason you are carrying out a piece of research is to take children's voices seriously, then your research will have a child-centred methodology. This child-centred methodology will inform the questions that you ask, the literature that you read, the methods you use and how you analyse your data (Clough and Nutbrown, 2007). Thus your methodology, that is, your principles and values concerning your topic, informs the entire research process.

Some research stories

When reading the following personal research stories, ask yourself the following questions:

- How are the researcher's personal and professional issues combined?
- What drives and motivates the researcher to carry out their research?
- What are the researcher's underpinning methodologies?

Katy's personal research story

I live in London and my boyfriend is Jamaican and a lot of our friends are African and West Indian. I'm really interested in the different ways in which black and white children learn about their identities. How do children learn their racial identity? This is my personal interest. My friends' kids are so aware of race even though they're little, you know, 3- and 4-year-olds. They're really interested in the colour of my skin and their skin. They'll say my skin is white or peachy and that they have brown skin. I'm really interested in these children's knowledge. Nurseries and schools are really really important in helping children to learn their racial identity so that's why I'm doing my project! There was also a really good lecture on race here and that made me think even more about how important multi-cultural education is. I'll probably work in London as a social worker on a SureStart project in a mixed area and it's important that I understand everything I can about these issues and be knowledgeable about the latest research. So this research project will be really good for my career.

Katy's methodology

Katy's research project is closely connected to her social situation and hence is meaningful and important to her. Katy's research is motivated by her concern with issues of social justice for ethnic minority children in early years settings. Her values and principles come from a deeply held conviction about the injustice of racism, especially when directed towards children. Thus her methodologies underpinning the research are child-centred and anti-racist (Siraj-Blatchford and Clarke, 2000).

Lucy's personal research story

Lucy's research concerned women and children and domestic violence. The ethics of this difficult and sensitive issue meant that Lucy's research was limited to asking professionals about domestic violence. Clearly, for a novice researcher first-hand research with the victims of domestic violence was not appropriate.

> When I was little I had a violent father. I have grown up hating violence. I am now so interested in this topic that I will be reading about it in the summer after I have handed my research study in. I am emotionally strong enough to carry out this research since I have gone through counselling and it was years ago. I have a family of my own now and have discussed it with my children. I feel very strongly about the issue. I feel it's something I really want to further investigate. I want to know what laws and policies and practices are in place to prevent domestic violence from occurring. What do schools, if anything, tell children about domestic violence? I want to help in some way because I am a survivor and am now in a position to help other victims. So I want to have more knowledge about the problem. The research is not just about therapy for me, although inevitably there is a bit of that too, but rather so I can improve my knowledge and get a job in the area. I'm quite determined to do this. My research has shown me that the children's viewpoints of domestic violence are often overlooked in all this. Also that professionals working with children are often unsure about domestic violence.

Lucy's methodology

Through the research Lucy wished to develop her self-understanding and raise the awareness about domestic violence amongst professionals working with children. The human rights of women and children to be free from violence and fear drive her research. Lucy's methodology is thus feminist and child-centred. These deeply held values informed her reading, methods and analysis of her research.

Mark's personal research story

In my research I wanted to find out about how other men experience the early childhood setting. I'm disabled and doing this course has proved to me and to others that I've been able to overcome my health difficulties. I've proved to people that my health is not an issue and now I find that I have got to prove that my gender is not an issue. It's funny really 'cos I knew that my health issues would be a struggle but I never thought that my gender would be a struggle.

This research project is good preparation for my own working life as a man in the early years. What prejudices does society hold about men in the early years and how do other men deal with such prejudices? The research project has made me feel more knowledgeable and wised up about being a man in the early years. Hopefully it will now be a bit easier to cope with. I've found out about other men's personal opinions and achievements despite the prejudices and this has really grabbed me. I've just got drawn into some articles and books which are so interesting that I just want to find out more.

Mark's methodology

Mark's personal research story centres around his identity as a disabled man who wants to work with young children. The political context of his research is concerned with gender and disability equality in the early years. His underpinning methodology is gender awareness within the early years and inclusion of people with physical impairments (Booth and Ainscow, 2004). The research has provided Mark with insight into the stereotypes that exist about men in the early years. With the knowledge gained from his research Mark feels more knowledgeable and confident about being a man working in the early years.

Sarah's research story

I worked in a play scheme and I thought that the friendships that the children formed were really fascinating. These 2- and 3-year-old children came in, not knowing each other and yet quickly some of them got on with each other very well. These young children made such strong friendships in such a short space of time. They looked forward to seeing each other every day and if someone was away they would ask after them! I found it amazing to watch. I can clearly remember an incident in which I was trying to comfort Anna, a 2-year-old girl, who had just started nursery. Maisy, another 2-year-old girl who hadn't been at the nursery very long herself, came up to us and gave Anna a big hug saying 'wants mummy'. I found the ability to empathise at this early age and the desire to help each other quite fascinating. I remember a lecturer quoting from Piaget saying that toddlers were egocentric and didn't empathise. Well this wasn't my experience! It made me want to read more about young children and friendships. I mean how do they learn to get along so quickly like this? It was so interesting to see.

I also worked in a school and saw some children who had poor self-esteem and who didn't have many friends. I was interested in that too. So my general topic of interest focused upon friendship which seems to be so important for children and their emotional well-being.

This research has given me an insight into the emotional development of children's friendships and how sociable children really are. I would like to be a family counsellor but in the short term I want to work for a charity that helps children and their families.

Sarah's methodology

Sarah's work experience has shown her that young children can empathise with other young children's emotional states at a very young age. She finds this 'fascinating' particularly because it contradicts what she heard in a lecture about toddlers being egocentric and unable to empathise. Sarah has a deeply held conviction about the social competencies and social abilities of young children. This child-centred research methodology led her to use participatory and child-centred research methods which listened to and took seriously children's perspectives and viewpoints (Lancaster and Broadbent, 2003).

Gail's personal research story

My son is in a Reception class at the moment so that's a strong motivation to look at this topic. I'm hoping that in the future learning will be an enjoyable thing for my son because at the moment he absolutely hates school.

I am a really strong believer in play. I have worked for many years in a nursery and have seen how children benefit from play. I think my son hates school because there is not enough emphasis on play. I just don't believe in Reception class that they should be made to hold pencils and taught to write on worksheets. I have an issue with worksheets and they use them every day at my son's school. I just don't agree with this. They should be learning about themselves as learners. All children should be doing stuff to build their self-esteem and social skills and get all the basic skills before they move on. Play is children's natural way of doing this.

The philosophy behind the Foundation Stage Curriculum Guidance seems to be brilliant. It is play based, but the philosophy is only as good as the people who implement it. With my research I was trying to make the practitioners aware of their practice. It's really important that teachers reflect upon their practice. So my research was about encouraging this reflection and for the teachers to see what they were doing. I wanted them to know that I knew what they were supposed to be doing with my son. I really wanted them not to do the worksheets with my son.

Soon after, I read an article on children's perceptions of school and what they thought school was for and what work and play were. This triggered my ideas off and made me realise that I could do research into this area. Before I read this article I wasn't sure if I could do this research or not.

Gail's methodology

Children's rights, including a child's right to play, is the social justice issue at the heart of Gail's study. Gail is centrally concerned with the happiness of her son as he starts school in Reception class. From her experience and reading she believes that young children like her son should be learning crucially important social and emotional skills through play rather than be pushed into formal learning at too early an age. Gail's passionately held beliefs in children's rights to play led her research to be underpinned by a child-centred methodology.

Your reflective diary

It is important to carry out such personal reflection on your own and in your own time. Your personal motivations are part of generating the methodology, validity and authenticity of the research project. To begin with give yourself 20 minutes to scribble down any autobiographical ideas that come into your head. Over the course of a few days and weeks revisit the areas of personal interest in your life and see how these issues connect together. This can be done with a handwritten diary or on the computer. Such notes can be kept and begin to make up your personal research diary. Such a personal and confidential research diary will help you in the process of formulating a meaningful research topic and research questions.

Add into your diary the discussions you have had with family and friends and work colleagues about children in your centre, and possibly your own children. Much high-quality early childhood research begins with the researcher's own children. You may have observed something with the children at your centre or school which really interests you. Perhaps you and your work colleagues and friends and family have been discussing a particular early childhood issue which has fired your interest and you would like to know more about it. Try to look out for the connections between these observations and your autobiography.

The mass media of television, newspapers, magazines, radio and the Internet is constantly reporting and creating childhood crises and concerns. In your research diary you should try to keep note of any such articles or programmes which you have been particularly interested in. If you are a student, you may have heard something in a lecture or seminar which you would like to follow up.

With all the above different inputs into your research diary you should try to keep yourself and your deep personal motivations centre stage. Try to see how the other inputs from work colleagues, family and friends, lectures, the media and books build upon *your* personal interests. You come first, not the other way around!

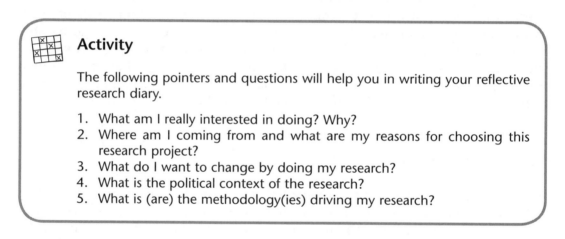

Activity

The following pointers and questions will help you in writing your reflective research diary.

1. What am I really interested in doing? Why?
2. Where am I coming from and what are my reasons for choosing this research project?
3. What do I want to change by doing my research?
4. What is the political context of the research?
5. What is (are) the methodology(ies) driving my research?

Some of what you write might be confidential, in which case do not share it with anybody else. Do be aware of the ethical issues concerned with research, which are discussed in Chapter 4. Due to the sensitive ethical nature of early childhood there are some topics which are not ethically possible to research. You might find it useful to share some edited versions of your story with a friend, and possibly your tutor. You might want to edit and develop further some of what you have written for inclusion in the written project itself.

High levels of motivation

It is important that your research project is personally meaningful for you because you will need high levels of motivation to complete your research project successfully. It is this enthusiasm and the desire to know that keeps Gail up at night and gets her out of bed early on a wet Monday morning! Such motivation will encourage you to work hard, as Gail records:

> If I was doing something I really wasn't interested in I wouldn't have the heart to sit there and read a book about it – 'cos I'm so interested I want to read about it. If you're really interested in it you don't mind sitting there at 10.00 at night reading a book – you want to know. I send everybody out, including the dog, so I can read! It is such an interesting issue. You really have to be passionate and fascinated and want to make a difference.

Gail wanted her research project to make a difference for her son and her own understanding of the issues of play in early childhood education. Some researchers such as Gail are seeking enhanced clarity around issues that they have long had a personal interest in. Many researchers wish to gain insight into the area that they are researching in order to develop themselves in some way. Such personal change can lead to enhanced self-confidence and self-esteem flowing from enhanced insight. An enhanced confidence in the area of their interest might lead to job applications in that particular area. Lucy, who looked at the issue of domestic violence, initially wanted to be a teacher:

> but that's not for me now. This research has given me the confidence to apply for jobs in the area of domestic violence. I now want to work as a domestic violence officer co-ordinating an educational initiative. When I go for interview I know what to say and what questions to ask. This project has really helped me when I start work.

Lucy's research project, which had deep personal meaning for her, had developed her insight and confidence into the area so much that she was now applying for jobs in the area of domestic violence and preventative educational projects.

Professional motivations

Be selfish with your choice of research topic. Choose a topic which will be of benefit to your career. You are investing a tremendous amount of time and resources into your research project. Make the research count and work for you. If you know the area of early childhood in which you wish to pursue your career, try to arrange to have a meeting with someone in that profession: a nurse, a teacher, a SureStart project worker, a nursery manager. Ask them what areas of early childhood need researching from their professional point of view. Lucy's research focused upon a range of early childhood professionals' understandings of domestic violence. This knowledge helped her to secure a job as a domestic violence education officer. If you hope to become an early years teacher, choose an educational topic and appropriate Key Stage setting. If you wish to become a speech and language therapist, choose to study an issue within this topic in the appropriate setting. If you wish to work in some aspect of the SureStart projects then choose to study an area of this major government project in its context.

If the professionals' ideas fit with your personal interests, then wonderful. If your personal ideas are different from their professional needs then perhaps you can work out a compromise. If you are a further/higher education student then you must discuss your research topic with your tutor and supervisor. Your tutor can often build upon your ideas for your research topic and possibly suggest career pathways.

Activity

As you think strategically about your career, answer the following questions:

What areas of early childhood would you like to work in when you complete your course?
How can your research project further your career?
What work opportunities might arise as a consequence of your research?
Have you seen your college/university tutor?
Have you chatted with a professional in the area?
Have you talked your research ideas through with your family and friends?

Focusing on your area of interest

One of the most important ways of finding the specific area you wish to investigate is to read relevant articles and books, check websites, view television documentaries, reflect upon your work experiences and talk through your ideas with your friends, family and tutor. All these information sources are essential so you can begin to formulate opinions and views on key issues within your topic area. From your reading and discussions different ideas will emerge and you will see just how complex your topic area is. New possibilities and interests within the topic area will keep opening up. At this early stage in the research process such new ideas and avenues within your wider topic area are to be welcomed. As a result of your reading and discussions your specific focus may shift and change. Further reflection within your research diary may lead you to change your focus again. Such creative shifts in the focus of your research are normal and healthy and a creative part of the research process.

Once you have decided upon your general topic of interest you should try to focus upon a specific area. At some point within the process of exploring your general topic area you will have to make a decision about what it is you *specifically* intend to research. A good research study has a particular and specific focus. When starting your research it is easy to go off on many different interesting routes around your research ideas. This is valid and healthy but your work can rapidly lose focus. Many interrelated areas connect with childhood studies, such as education, health, sociology and anthropology. Each area has its own literature and interest in childhood. It is important, therefore, that your personal study area is as focused as possible. Five stages can be identified in this focusing process.

1. Identify the general area in which you are interested.

2. Read, read, read in the general area – find out what others have said and done in your area.

3. Reflect upon your work experiences and talk your ideas through with your family, friends and tutors.

4. Carry out a pilot study.

5. Try to identify the specific issues within this area that you are interested in.

In the following case study identify the general area that Sam is considering researching.

- What are the four specific issues that Sam could research?

- Is Sam's research sufficiently focused?

- Do you think this is a problem at this early stage?

- What should Sam do in order to focus her research?

Case study

Sam worked part time in a Reception classroom as a teaching assistant at a local primary school. She was also enrolled to do a childhood studies degree and had to carry out a small-scale research project. Sam has three brothers and has always been interested in issues of gender at home and now at work. Whilst at work Sam wondered why so many boys played with the Lego whilst the girls choose to play in the home corner. This interest in gender issues was confirmed at college by a stimulating lecture on gender and childhood. She began to read in the area of gender and became fascinated in the 'nature nurture' debate. Why did boys and girls act so differently at such an early age? Back at work Sam became more interested in the gendered aspects of her work. Why were all the classroom assistants and teachers female except for the male headteacher? She spoke to her friends at other schools and this confirmed that there was only one man in the early years in the town. She wondered why this might be.

At playtimes Sam observed how boys and girls would often choose to play in separate gender groups. She found some articles on the Internet about children and friendship groups and became very interested in gender and friendship and what the connection might be.

In the classroom Sam had noticed how some of the girls seemed to be much more interested in reading books and writing stories than did some of the boys. She knew that the girls' interest in reading and writing in Reception was connected with girls doing better at tests in Year 2 and Year 6 of the primary school. She had a hunch that this was to do with the lack of positive male role models in the boys' lives and wanted to find out more about the boys' home lives. Sam was interested in finding out about school policies and practices that were in place to get boys more interested in literacy.

In the above case study Sam is going through the normal process of talking and reading as she attempts to specifically identify the focus of her research topic. Sam has decided that her general interest is in the area of gender. Through her work experiences, chatting with friends, and library and Internet literature searching she has developed many related gender interests:

- gender and friendship
- gender and literacy
- gender and inclusion issues throughout the school
- teachers' gender and career issues.

Each of the above issues is so big that they could be the worthwhile study of four separate investigations in their own right. Sam must focus upon exactly which of the above gender issues she will pursue further.

After further reading and reflection at work, and discussions with her tutor, Sam decided to focus her interest upon gender and friendship groups. She made this choice because the other issues were too big for the six-month time frame allowed for her project. She had a good relationship with the children and wished the study to focus upon children's gender and their friendship groups.

 Activity

Look at the general research area that you are interested in. Now try to make this general research area more focused and specific to one particular issue.

What is it exactly that you wish to find out more about?

Complete these sentences:

In my research study I wish to find out more about ...
I want to look at this specific issue because ...

Writing your research questions will help you to focus your interest of study on a specific area.

The overall research questions and the field questions

There are two main types of questions in research. The overall research questions structure and frame the research project and, to a certain extent, are answered by the whole project. This chapter is concerned with these large overarching general questions of the study which define and clarify the limits of your study. The field questions are the actual, specific detailed questions that the researcher asks people in interviews and on questionnaires. Chapters 6, 7, 8 and 9 look at the more detailed questions which you actually ask people in the early childhood setting. These field questions are used later in the study to collect evidence for your project to answer the overall research questions.

The large overall research questions are important because they:

- define the limits and context of your study
- clarify the purposes of the study

- help to concentrate and focus your thinking, reading and writing upon the specific area

- help to clarify the methods – that is, sort out what you actually need to do

- keep your research going in the right direction for the duration of the study.

Getting your research questions right – breadth and depth

It is a difficult but important task for the researcher to make their research questions 'just right' (Clough and Nutbrown, 2007). Getting the balance of making your research questions sufficiently broad to make your work interesting and at the same time focused enough so that you can actually answer the questions in your short time-frame, is quite a skill.

A good research study has specific and doable research questions. Your research questions will keep bringing you back to exactly what it is you are looking at in your work. The wonderful thing about good research questions is that they will help your work to have both breadth and depth. On the one hand, your research questions need to be sufficiently broad to engage with the wider political and social context of your work. Your research study needs these wider connections to make your study relevant, significant and interesting. On the other hand, the questions must be specific and detailed so as to ensure depth and clarity of purpose in your work. Such specific questions will help to ensure that your work does not ramble. Your questions also need to be doable and realistic for you to answer within your limited timescale. When your tutor finally marks your work, he/she will be looking to see whether or not your study has answered your overall research questions. Writing specific and doable research questions is a process. In the light of your ongoing reading and discussions they will shift and change.

Activity

Do your research questions allow your work to be sufficiently broad to engage with the wider issues?

Are your research questions specific and focused enough to avoid your work being rambling and disconnected?

Look back again at Sam's case study. The following demonstrates questions that are too big or too small, and those that may be considered just right for Sam's purposes.

Sam's research topic on gender and literacy

Three research questions which are too big:

1. Why do the boys not read very much and why do the girls read a lot?

2. Why do girls do so much better at tests in the school?

3. What sort of things do boys like doing at school?

These questions are too big because they do not define the limits of the study. They are unfocused. The context for the research has not been established. Which boys and girls, and whereabouts are they located? The questions also carry assumptions concerning *all* boys and *all* girls, and such issues have not yet been established. The third question does not relate to the first two.

Three questions which are too small:

1. Is Jack a good reader because his father is a teacher and reads with him at home every night?

2. What impact upon Jack's reading was there after reading a football magazine with him?

3. Is the fact that Jack is left-handed significant for his literacy development?

These questions are clearly too small to be of sustained interest over a period of time. The questions focus upon one boy and make assumptions about his literacy development. The project would have more validity if it encompassed a wider range of children and viewpoints. The final question focuses upon one literacy event and ignores the girls.

Three questions which are specific and doable:

1. How do all the various stakeholders within the children's centre understand the term 'literacy'?

2. Within the children's centre what are the variety of contexts for literacy events?

3. What similar and different literacy events do boys and girls participate in?

The first question opens up the concept of literacy. This question allows all the members of the school – the children, the teachers and the parents – to define how they understand literacy. It is an inclusive question and begins to point towards the methods of actually collecting the evidence for the study. The second question allows the study to explore what literacy events occur within the children's centre. This question encourages the researcher to observe and critically watch what goes on in a Foundation Stage classroom. It is a sufficiently broad question to allow the researcher to make connections from many observed relationships and activities towards an inclusive definition of literacy. The third question focuses upon the gender issue. Only after having established what literacy is and why, and in what contexts it occurs, can we focus upon gender and literacy. The question pointedly states that there will be similar and different literacy activities with the boys and girls. This question will prevent the researcher from making generalisations about all boys and all girls.

 Activity

Now try to write three or four specific questions for your research topic. Remember that writing research questions is an ongoing process and will take several attempts until you are completely confident of them.

For each question that you write:

- Reflect upon whether it is too big or too small until you feel that it is 'just right'.
- Go through your questions and ask yourself 'What do I need to do to find an answer to this question?' In this way you will begin to identify the actual tasks that could be done to answer each question, for example, library research, questionnaires, interviews, observations, diaries, drawings and photographs.

Doing a pilot study

A pilot study often involves gathering evidence and information from people before you carry out the larger study. A pilot study can help to check that your research topic and research questions and planning are going along the right lines (Figure 2.1). A pilot study is critical at the beginning of your study because it will alert you as to whether or not your research questions, approaches and

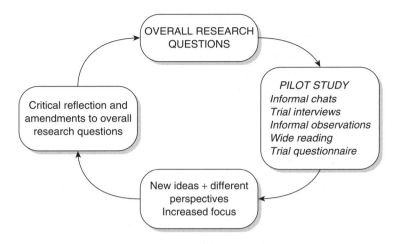

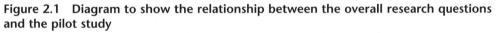

Figure 2.1 Diagram to show the relationship between the overall research questions and the pilot study

proposed research methods are specific, ethical and actually doable. In the light of the findings of your pilot study, your research questions and plan might well need refining and rephrasing with some changes. Such changes to your plan must be seen as a positive step because a pilot study is concerned with reflecting upon and revisiting your work to date.

Lucy's pilot study

For her pilot study Lucy had informal chats with two teacher friends and a domestic violence officer about her research project. She also trialled her interview questions. She needed to do this to clarify in her mind what the field questions would be for her survey questionnaires. Lucy was interested to note that in each of three open-ended discussions remarkably similar issues arose. Lack of adequate training and knowledge as to how to respond to children who were experiencing domestic violence was an unexpected recurrent theme. These and other issues formed the basis of the themes asked about in her questionnaires which she then sent out. In addition she then trialled the questionnaires themselves.

Sarah's pilot study

Sarah's pilot study included a series of observations in the classroom in which she was to carry out her research on friendships. As Sarah watched and talked through her plans with the classroom, she realised that she would have to be much more focused in her topic. She observed that friendships in the classroom were based upon a whole range of issues including socio-economic class, race, gender, children's self-esteem, age, networks outside school, the teacher's planning and responses to children, physical disability and ability. Although each of these issues contributed to children's friendship in some way, Sarah needed to focus upon just one issue. She chose the issue 'friendship and gender' for her focus. However, Sarah was aware that the issues mentioned above might be equally as important as gender and acknowledged this as a limitation within her study.

Such pilot observations also served the purpose of helping the children to build up a relationship with Sarah and learn to trust her. Sarah's pilot study reinforced what she had read about children perceiving her as a teacher and how this would impinge upon the children's spontaneity in discussions with her. This realisation led her to adopt drawings as a research method, since the children seemed freely and spontaneously to draw when given the opportunity. Hence the importance of the pilot study in alerting her to more appropriate research methods.

Summary

This chapter has:

- provided the reasons as to why you need to think passionately with your heart and strategically with your head when planning the area you wish to research

- discussed the central importance of keeping a reflective personal diary

- discussed the critical role of research questions in helping you to focus upon a specific issue

- demonstrated the ways to write focused overall research questions.

Recommended reading

Clough, P. and Nutbrown, C. (2007) *A Student's Guide to Methodology*. London: Sage Publications.

Chapters 1 and 2 provide sound arguments for your work being personal and making connections with wider political issues. These two chapters provide compelling case studies for reflecting upon your personal learning journey by doing research.

Reed, M. and Canning, N. (eds) (2009) *Reflective Practice in the Early Years.* London: Sage Publications.

This book is organised into four sections which link closely to the principles of the Early Years Foundation Stage. It provides a useful resource on how to work reflectively with the EYFS and contains many examples and case studies that could be developed into research projects.

3

Ethical issues in early childhood research

Learning objectives

This chapter will help you to:

- understand that ethical principles should continuously permeate all aspects of your research
- understand how children's rights legislation affects your research
- appreciate the balance between children's participation and children's protection
- carry out an 'impact assessment on children' of your proposed research
- reflect upon your responsibilities as an ethical researcher.

Legislation and the participatory rights of children

Seeing children as valuable participants in the research process has come about as a result of legislation and changing sociological perspectives (Christensen and James, 2008). Today's research ethical codes and practices find their roots in the Nuremberg Code (1949) which was established in response to the Nazis' research atrocities in concentration camps. The Nuremberg Code stipulates:

- The absolute *necessity* for voluntary consent of research subjects.
- The need to ensure that the research is for the good of society.
- Any unnecessary physical and mental suffering to be avoided.
- Assessment of any potential risks to the research subjects.
- The necessity of allowing research subjects to withdraw from the research at any stage of the process (Greig and Taylor, 1999: 147).

The United Nations *Convention on the Rights of the Child* (UNCRC) (UN, 1989) provides a framework for addressing rights relating to children's need for care, protection and adequate provision, *and* on children's rights to participation (Taylor, 2000: 25). It aims to protect and promote children's rights and welfare through a set of principles made up of 54 legally binding articles. Article 12 of the Convention is the most significant for research purposes because it declares that children have the right to hold an opinion about issues concerning them: 'State parties shall assure to the child who is capable of forming his or her own views the right to express those views freely in all matters affecting the child' (UN, 1989: Article 12). Hence children have the right to be included in research which affects them. Although lacking legal status in the UK, Article 12 was ratified by the UK government in 1991, and clearly represents a major cultural shift towards the recognition of children as full participating members of society in the same way that adults are. It requires that adults respect the rights of children. As regards research, Article 12 means that 'children have the right to be consulted and taken account of, to have access to information, to freedom of speech and opinion and to challenge decisions made on their behalf' (Morrow and Richards, 1996: 91).

At the same time as encouraging their participation, the UNCRC recognises that children are vulnerable, by placing the child's right to participate alongside their right for protection. The UNCRC demands a cultural shift away from working *for* children to working *with* children since the power balance between adults and children has shifted in favour of children (Kirby et al., 2003). Such an objective has been given impetus by the Children Bill (DfES, 2004) and the role of the Children's Commissioner. Specifically, the Commissioner,

> has a duty to *proactively consult children* and young people, involve them in his work, seek out their opinions, particularly the opinions of those children who would not normally be given a voice, and encourage persons engaged in activities related to children to take account of these views. (Harvey, 2004: 4, emphasis added.)

Thus the Children Bill (DfES, 2004) represents a further major legislative impetus in listening to and acting upon children's voices and opinions in research. It encourages those who work and research with young children to listen to the voices of children and to ensure that they participate in the research process.

Soon after the UNCRC (UN, 1989) the British government passed the Children Act (1989). Like the UNCRC the Children Act established that children should have the right to be heard about matters affecting their welfare. Both the UNCRC and the Children Act have had considerable impact upon any research concerned with children because they encourage the participation of children in the research process. Similarly at the heart of the Early Years Foundation Stage (DCSF, 2008) is a commitment to respecting and listening to the varied voices and viewpoints of young children.

Sociology and the participatory rights of children

Children have, until relatively recently, been seen through the lens of deficit and social pathology. Children's social competencies and their abilities were negated within a pathological model of childhood which centred upon their low chronological age. Hence, children's needs and wants were interpreted by the adults around them, who spoke for children. Young children were seen as lacking in social competency and insight. Indeed, children were constructed not as human *beings* but rather as human *becomings* (Quortrup, 1987). Children could only gain social competency once they were fully developed adults. Thus within this negative model of childhood, that is, what children *cannot* do, children were perceived as having little of significance and importance to offer the research process.

Increasingly, children are viewed as socially competent and as 'experts in their own lives' (Langsted, 1994). It is seen as imperative that researchers should include children's understandings and experiences in studies which may affect children (Kirby et al., 2003). Indeed, researchers working with children are actively encouraged to *listen* to children and to take their views seriously. Malaguzzi (1996: 10) suggests that children are 'rich in potential, strong, powerful, competent and, most of all, connected to adults and other children'.

Ethics is centrally concerned with the attitudes of the researcher. If the researcher's attitude is one of respect for children's abilities, then the researcher is likely to use a variety of methods to listen to children's voices.

> If we, adults, think of children as powerful, they act powerful. If we treat them as powerful, they rise to our expectations. Indeed they can blow the tops of our heads off in terms of what they can do, if we choose to stand aside and let them, and see them in their true colours. (Drummond, 2002: 3)

Question: In what ways does your research project allow children to surprise and astound you with their abilities and social competency?

Children's participation and protection

The complex relationship in research with children between their *participation*, on the one hand, and their *protection* from risk, on the other hand, *must* be given due consideration by the researcher (Coady, 2010: 68). The impact of participation upon children may have all sorts of institutional and personal benefits for the children. However, it is essential that the researcher is reflective throughout to ensure that the impact *is* beneficial and not causing the child unnecessary stress and anxiety.

All research carries with it the *potential* for risk amongst the research participants, both children and adults, and for the researcher themselves (Coady, 2010). Such risk is often *inadvertent* because, clearly, the researcher does not set out to emotionally upset people but, despite the best of intentions, such emotional upset may occur. However well intended, research questions can and do touch upon sensitive issues for children and adults. Children can be made to feel quite vulnerable by questions which intrude upon their personal relationships with their families and friends. Researchers with the best of intentions might by accident frighten and worry children by stirring up issues and events that are difficult for them. Questions might make the child think there is a problem with them and/or their family. Children are particularly vulnerable to difficult questions when the researcher is unfamiliar with them and their lives (Lancaster and Broadbent, 2010).

Whilst encouraging children's participation in the research process, it does need to be noted that some research projects carry with them the potential for negative impacts upon children. One such possible negative impact is the invasion of children's privacy by enquiring adults. It is an irony that the more imaginative and sensitive researchers become to listening to children, the greater the possibility of further intruding into their private worlds (Clark et al., 2003: 27). Thus, participatory research might be seen by children as yet another form of observation and surveillance of their lives by controlling adults.

A further concern is that researchers who rush to engage with the participation agenda might use disempowering research techniques such as one-to-one interviews and questionnaires. Asking children to engage with such inappropriate methods might lead to confirmation of the myth that young children cannot participate in research (Alderson, 2008). A further potential negative impact of participatory research is that it might be perceived by the children as tokenistic. Tokenistic participatory research projects have little or no action following consultation with children. The problem with such research is that children might soon become disillusioned with the nature of participation if they perceive that what they say is subsequently ignored in practice (Kirby et al., 2003).

It is the responsibility of the ethical researcher to ensure that any such risk is *minimised*. One possible way of doing this is through the process of carrying out an impact assessment. The objective of an impact assessment on children is to encourage the researcher to be critically reflective about any aspects of the research which might lead to upsetting any of the participants, especially the children.

A reflective impact assessment of research on children

Several professional bodies such as the National Children's Bureau (NCB, 2003) (http://www.ncb.org.uk/dotpdf/.../research_guidelines_200604.pdf) have ethical guidelines, based upon the Nuremberg Code, which seek to protect children and the researcher. Colleges and universities have ethical guidelines and ethical committees which are based upon such professional codes and guidelines. If your research project is being carried out for a qualification through a college, then your research plans must be scrutinised according to your college's ethical guidelines. Your ethical discussion will show the readers of your report that you are aware of your ethical responsibilities regarding your respondents' participation and protection.

The following questions can be used to help organise your thinking and writing concerning ethical issues in your research.

- What potentially sensitive issues are raised by your research questions?

- What are the various ways in which your research questions might be inadvertently taken the wrong way?

- How might your questions cause the research respondent to worry in any way after you have finished?

- Could your research questions inadvertently have any negative impact upon relationships within the early childhood institution?

- Could your research questions inadvertently have any negative impact upon family relationships?

- In what ways does your research make the institution and its members vulnerable to potential criticism?

- What advantages to the respondents and their early childhood institution might there be from your research?

If you are concerned about any of the above questions, perhaps you should reconsider your research questions. If you are feeling that your questions might make children vulnerable in any way, then it might be preferable not to work with children as respondents this time. Perhaps because of your relative research inexperience you might consider carrying out a particular piece of research at a later stage. Some inexperienced first-time researchers who are wary about upsetting children include children's voices *by proxy* in their research. That is, they do not carry out the research with the children themselves but, rather, refer to literature in which such research with children has already been carried out. If you choose to incorporate the voices of children by proxy then you can state in your report why you are doing so. Lucy's research with domestic violence included the voices of children by proxy and is discussed later.

Your emotional vulnerability

As discussed in Chapter 2, research can be introspective and may unconsciously focus upon unresolved personal issues (West, 1996). Generally, for the inexperienced researcher the best advice is to stick to research topics which are relatively emotionally safe. Any potential risks can be minimised early on at the planning stage of the research. There may be the odd occasions where both you and your supervisor feel you can proceed with an emotionally difficult subject. Lucy's research, for example, was concerned with the issue of domestic violence.

When Lucy went to her research supervisor with the suggestion that she investigate the issue of domestic violence, her supervisor was understandably initially concerned. As a mature woman with her own family, Lucy explained that over the years she had come to terms with the domestic violence she had experienced as a child and had forgiven her now dead parents. Nevertheless, Lucy stated that she was aware of the potential emotional risks involved for her in the research and reflected upon her emotional state throughout the research. Her research supervisor made the decision that Lucy was sufficiently reflective and mature to proceed with the research.

📁 Case study: Ethically reflective research with children

Initially Katy, a white woman, had wanted to talk with her friends' children about their racial identities. Her friends' children were black British and mixed heritage and she knew some of the children quite well. However, upon critical reflection of her research questions Katy felt that the research could potentially and inadvertently upset some of the children. Katy had read that fostering and developing a positive, healthy and strong racial identity amongst children can be an emotionally complex and sensitive issue (Siraj-Blatchford and Clarke, 2000). Upon reflection she realised that she did not know the families as well as she thought she did and was concerned that she might inadvertently intrude upon complex family situations and dynamics. She also considered how the research questions might leave the children anxious and questioning about their identities when previously they might never have considered them to be an issue. She also became aware that as a white woman she did not have the same racial experience and insight of a black woman or man. A black person might be more sensitive in fostering and encouraging a positive and confident self-image amongst the children. After critically reflecting upon these issues, Katy realised that her research could have the opposite effect of her intentions; that is, the research might inadvertently undermine the children and make them more vulnerable and anxious concerning their developing sense of self and racial identity. She realised that perhaps a more experienced researcher might be more appropriate in this instance.

Katy decided to examine the ways in which two nurseries promoted the children's ethnic identities. Rather than focusing upon the children, with all its associated potential for risk, the research was to now focus upon the institutions and what they were doing to encourage children's racial identities. Taking the spotlight away from the children and focusing it upon the nurseries' staff, curriculum and resources *minimised* the risk to the children. As a result of their adult power and professionalism the practitioners in the nurseries were less vulnerable than the children to any inadvertent harm.

However, Katy noted in her research report that, because 'race' is a politically important topic, nurseries might feel threatened by her research. Nurseries are now inspected by the Office for Standards in Education (OFSTED) to see that they are in accordance with the Race Relations Act 2001, in which nurseries, along with other educational institutions, have a duty actively to *promote* the development of children's racial and cultural identities. Katy appreciated that the nurseries, by allowing her in to do research in this area, were potentially making the institution and therefore themselves vulnerable to any criticism. Katy therefore assured the nurseries of the utmost importance of confidentiality and that the institutions would not be recognisable in her report. She made it clear to the managers and teachers that her research was primarily concerned with her learning about how the nursery successfully promoted children's racial and cultural identities. By unequivocally stating that the research report was for her and her college tutor, Katy sought to minimise the nurseries' apprehension and she successfully gained access to the two nurseries to carry out her research.

Lucy was aware that, with such a sensitive subject, direct research with the victims of domestic violence was clearly not an option. Hence, Lucy did not carry out any direct research with the victims of domestic violence. Her study was limited to professionals, including nursery practitioners, teachers, family liaison officers, social workers and domestic violence officers. Such professionals have the necessary distance, objectivity and professional training to discuss such sensitive issues.

Lucy wanted to include children's perspectives on domestic violence in her research report and these she gained *by proxy* from the literature and the Internet. This method of including children's voices by proxy is useful for inexperienced researchers when investigating sensitive subjects. If you have concerns about the ethical implications of carrying out research with children, this method of including children's voices by proxy from the literature is a safe alternative.

Informed consent

Informed consent refers to the research participants *voluntarily agreeing* to participate in a research project based upon complete disclosure of all relevant information and the recipient's understanding of this (www.ncb.org.uk/ dotpdf/.../research_guidelines_200604.pdf). Gaining the participants' informed consent to carry out the research is part of building trust in the relationship between yourself and the research participants (Alderson, 2008). Trust requires that as a researcher you are honest, reliable and communicate all aspects of the research process to all the participants. The research participants have a right to know about the complete research process. Trust will develop over time as you honestly share your aims, methods and findings with the participants. The notion of informed consent, or *assent* as it is legally known with children, because they are deemed too immature to give informed consent, is central to the ethics of research. Careful thought needs to be given to translating this into practice when the research participant is a child. 'Do children understand the information that they have been given – in particular, how are very young children, children with learning disabilities, or children with communications problems to be informed and their consent gained?' (NCB, 2002: 3).

As a researcher you must ask yourself whether the children have been given all the information about the research that they need to make a decision as to whether to participate or not. Such a verbal explanation is best done with small groups of children or with individual children. Specifically, have you told the children in words that they can understand:

- what the research is about?
- what you hope to accomplish?
- their role?
- the benefits and consequences of participating in the research?
- what you will do with their views and any visuals that you take?
- how their views will be documented?
- how confidentiality will be upheld?
- the choice they have to consent or not to participate?
- the right they have to withdraw from the project at any time? (Lancaster and Broadbent, 2010: 15)

You must give the children time to discuss any questions that they may have concerning the above.

Informed consent, confidentiality and child protection

It is important that, *before* children and other research participants give their informed consent and actually participate in the research, they understand there is a *limit* to the anonymity and confidentiality that can be given to what they tell the researcher. This is due to child protection issues. The National Children's Bureau (2002) state the following:

> We believe that there must be limits to any guarantee of confidentiality or anonymity in situations where child protection is an issue. Where a child or young person divulges that they or others are at risk of significant harm or where the researcher observes or receives evidence of incidents likely to cause serious harm, the researcher has a *duty* to take steps to protect the child or other children. (NCB, 2002: 3)

In the above exceptional circumstances it is your *duty* as a researcher to inform the child that you will be telling a responsible adult, usually the key worker or the teacher and your college supervisor, what the child has told you. Thus there is a limit to the confidence which the researcher can keep. Respondents, including children and young people, should be told at the outset, and as necessary during the research, that confidentiality cannot be guaranteed if 'difficult' information arises. If, after discussion with the child, the researcher decides it is necessary to inform others – hopefully with the consent of the child – the researcher must ensure that the child has immediate support and is kept fully informed. You should also immediately discuss the situation with your college supervisor if any child protection issues arise.

 Activity

Read the following case study (Jane's) and answer these questions:

How did Jane fulfil her duties as a responsible and ethical researcher?
In what ways did Jane follow the National Children's Bureau's ethical guidelines (NCB, 2002)?

> ### Case study
>
> In Jane's research, which concerned understandings of childhood:
>
> > One child started to tell me about some abuse that was happening at home. I stopped the child immediately and said that if she wanted to continue to talk about it that I would need to talk to someone else about it as well. She was happy with this, and the information was passed on.
>
> Jane told the class teacher and her college supervisor and subsequently found out the girl was under close monitoring from the school and social services as a potential victim of domestic violence.
>
> > On another occasion I was very concerned about a boy's constant referral to death and dying – I did not have the skills to help him, and so again, with his permission I passed the information on to his class teacher. However, my ethical commitment did not end there, for it is important to ensure that something had been done.
>
> Jane was sensitive and realised that there may well be an unresolved emotional issue for this boy. With the boy's agreement she told his class teacher and her college supervisor. The teacher informed Jane that the child had recently suffered the particularly painful bereavement of his father. The school contacted the boy's mother and asked if the boy might like further counselling. Subsequently, the mother agreed and the boy received further bereavement counselling. Jane's compassionate sensitivity was of paramount importance in highlighting this boy's emotional needs.

Informed consent leaflet for children

When working with children, in addition to telling them about the research it is also good practice to produce a child-friendly leaflet outlining the research and what is expected of the children who choose to participate (Alderson, 2008). Older children will be able to read the leaflet on their own but younger children will need help, so it is a good idea to read it through with all the children whose parents/guardians gave permission for their child to participate in the research. Even if the children are not yet able to read the leaflet on their own, it is a good idea to write an information leaflet for children and to read it with them. Writing and talking through such a leaflet with children and adults will help you to think clearly about the nature and purpose of your work. This will improve the standard of your research and make it easier to explain to children and adults (Alderson,

2008). Writing and reading through the leaflet reproduced in the case study below with the children and adults involved in Jane's research was an important part of meeting her ethical obligations for the research.

As a corollary to the above inclusive and participatory research method, it is useful to remind ourselves what are *disrespectful* ethical methods of researching with children. Alderson (2008) gives an overview of such disrespectful methods. These include:

- Not respecting their privacy and confidentiality rights.

- Making covert observations, such as through one-way mirrors, secretly doing case studies, video and audio tapes.

- Discussing the children openly without altering their names or hiding their identity.

- Assuming that children are not yet able to speak for themselves.

- Asking adults (parents, teachers) for their views about a child's beliefs and behaviours but not also asking the child.

- Asking only negative and standard questions about children instead of also asking about each child's strengths, achievements and unique individuality.

- Using questionnaires with adult-centred questions such as 'What is your housing status?' that might make children look foolish.

- Labelling children without asking about their own reasons, which might make sense of their actions and views.

- Testing them in labs, without seeing that being in a strange place can unsettle and distract them and thereby lower their competencies.

- Routinely using upsetting methods, such as the tolerance of strangers test to see how babies react if their mother suddenly leaves them with a stranger.

- Using deception such as telling a child not to touch something, without giving any reason, then secretly watching them to see how long the child obeys.

- Talking down to children.

- Publishing results that reinforce negative stereotypes about children and young people. (Alderson, 2008)

Case study

Jane's research concerned perceptions of childhood today. She gave the following leaflet out to the children and read it through with all of them. After you have read the informed consent leaflet for children, try designing and writing such a leaflet for your research.

Research on childhood

This leaflet has been designed to try and answer some of the questions that you might want to ask. You may show this leaflet to your parent(s)/guardian if you wish, but you do not have to do so.

What is research?
Research is a bit like being a detective. It is about investigating a particular topic and collecting evidence so that you, and others, can know more about the topic. This will help people to understand the topic better.

What is the research about?
This can best be answered by giving you examples of *some* of the things we will be thinking about: What is childhood? At what age does childhood end? What are the best things about being a child? What are the worst things about being a child? What do you like doing? What don't you like doing? What are the differences between children and adults? In what ways are children and adults similar? Are you in a hurry to grow up?

Why have you been asked to take part?
I am not a child and so I don't really know what it is like to be a child today! The best people to tell me what childhood is like today are those who are experiencing it at the moment – you! On the topic of childhood you are the expert. Your views are therefore *very* important to me.

What will you be doing?
Three different activities have been planned:

(a) A questionnaire – this is a series of questions that asks for your thoughts on things to do with childhood. There will also be some diagrams to complete. This will be done on your own, in class. It is *not* a test. There are no right or wrong answers – it is just about what you think.
(b) Designing a poster about childhood. This will be done in small groups. You will be asked to look for things at home that you might use for your poster. Each group will discuss their poster with me.
(c) Talking with me about childhood. This will take place in small groups of two, three or four children. The aim of the talk will be to develop ideas and issues emerging from the questionnaires and posters.

Who else is involved in the research?
A questionnaire will be sent to your parent(s) to ask for their views about childhood. I am also looking at the newspapers, and the news on the radio and television, to see what they say about children and childhood.

Do you have to take part?
You will have the choice as to whether you want to take part in each activity but I hope that you will find it interesting and want to take part! It is an opportunity for *me* to learn from *you* and for you to put your views across.

Will anyone be told about what you say?
I will need to talk about the research with some people and I will also need to write about it, but no one (including your teacher and your parents) will ever be told who said what. Although it is unlikely, if you do tell me anything that really worries me, then we (you and I) will need to work out what to do about it.

Thank you for reading this! If you have any other questions then write them on the back of this leaflet and show them to me when you next see me.

(*Source*: Cox, 2005)

Using the disrespectful research methods listed on page 51, which adults would not accept, is likely to lead to poor research results. Not only is this a problem for the particular piece of research, but is in turn likely to reinforce negative stereotypes about children's competencies in research. Thus the unacceptable research methods above tend to perpetuate negative myths about children in research. In the following section respectful research practices with children are discussed.

Socially inclusive and respectful relationships with children

Clark (2004) states that listening to young children is central to ethics because:

- it acknowledges children's *right* for their views and experiences to be taken seriously about matters that affect them
- of the difference listening can make to our understanding of children's priorities, interests and concerns
- of the difference it can make to our understanding of how children feel about themselves
- listening is a vital part of establishing respectful relationships with the children we work with and is central to the learning process.

With a clearer understanding of children's lives, parents and practitioners are able to respond to the changes in children's lives, to meet their diverse needs and to improve care and services (Lancaster and Broadbent, 2010: 4). This does not mean that in the research process the perspectives of children are the sole 'voice' to be heard. Rather, listening to young children means that children's 'voices', alongside those of parents and practitioners, are to be included.

According to Lancaster and Broadbent (2010: 27), 'The starting point for listening to children is to form socially inclusive relationships'. The key to inclusive and ethical social relationships is to *respect* the child and this involves granting the young child social ability and intelligence. In a respectful research relationship the child is viewed as a person who has a valid and worthwhile perspective to offer on events that affect his/her life. In a respectful relationship the researcher does not limit and constrain the child's potential and possibility because of the child's young age.

Respectful research relationships, based upon informed consent, will go some way towards alleviating the power differences between the researcher and the child. However, it is important not to minimise the power held by the researcher. 'The biggest ethical challenge for researchers working with children is the disparities in power and status between adults and children' (Morrow and Richards, 1996: 98). Adults researching children carry power on the basis of their age relative to children and because of the unequal nature of much research (Mayall, 2000). Power that adults possess may also be related to the relationship between the adult and child, such as, parent, health worker, childcare worker or teacher, in which the adult has responsibility for the child in various ways. This relationship will affect the quality and reliability of the evidence produced. The ways in which children may provide answers they think the more powerful adult, such as a practitioner/researcher, wants to hear are discussed in Chapter 7.

Activity

In what ways do you hold power over the children you are carrying out research with?

Are your research questions and methods appropriate for the children?

How can your research methods challenge and question the power difference between adults and children?

How does gaining informed consent from children help to reduce the power differences between adult researchers and children?

In what other ways can you alleviate the power differences between yourself and the children?

Activity

The following questions are intended to problematise and provoke discussion concerning the issue of gaining informed consent with children. Informed consent with children is a difficult and problematic issue, and there are no clear-cut answers to the following questions. The answers must partly be dependent upon the context in which the research is being carried out.

How can the children be included in the research design?
How do we inform children about the research?
What are the ways in which informed assent can be gained with children?
How do we let children tell us that they no longer wish to participate with the research?
Do children feel they can tell us that they no longer wish to participate with the research?
How do we know that the children understand that they have the right to 'opt out' of the research if they choose?
What qualities are needed within the researcher–child relationship to allow the child the space to 'opt out' if they so choose?
Within a school context is it possible to alleviate the power differentials between adult researcher and child in order to allow for greater ownership of the research by the child?
How do we close the research?
Are the research findings to be presented with the children or to the children?
Will the research make a difference to the school and the children's lives?
How do we find out if action has been taken on the research outcomes?

Alderson (2008) asks the following questions concerning informed consent:

- Do we always have to obtain parents' as well as children's consent, even for older Year 6 children?

- Should we be barred from doing the research by parents' refusal when the children want to join the research?

- Is the headteacher's consent sufficient or ought we to ask every child in the school who might be observed?

- How do we research with whole classes, if one or two children object?

- How can we reduce the risks of children being coerced into joining a project?

- How can we reduce the risks of children being unwillingly excluded and silenced?

Informed consent is an ongoing process

Very young children may indicate that they like or dislike taking part in a research study in a number of different ways. Central to the UK's Early Years Foundation Stage (DCSF, 2008) is a commitment to listen to and respect young children's viewpoints. Informed consent, especially with young children, needs to be *continuously negotiated*. Informed consent is not a one-off event but, rather, a dynamic and subtle process (Martin, 2005). A child who wants to participate in the research one day, may change their mind the next day and may no longer wish to participate. This right *not* to participate on that particular occasion, frustrating though it might be to the researcher, has to be respected (Lancaster and Broadbent, 2010). In the following case study it can be seen how the research process and the children's participation were continuously negotiated.

Negotiating access with the gatekeepers

Gatekeepers are those professionals such as nursery managers, key workers, school teachers, headteachers and parents who can literally allow you entrance to the institution to carry out the research or who can forbid you from doing so. Such professionals act as gatekeepers both to their institutions and to the children who are their responsibility. In terms of whether you can do your research in the institution, the gatekeepers are very powerful people. Hence the importance of gaining the gatekeeper's consent and trust to carry out the research. You may also wish to interview and questionnaire the gatekeepers. So when seeking permission from gatekeepers, whether the nursery manager or the parents, it is important that they are provided with all relevant information about the research.

The institution may check with the parents or guardians that it is acceptable to carry out the research at the nursery or the school. It is not a legal requirement for a school or institution to do so since they are '*in loco parentis*'. In practice early childhood institutions often act '*in loco parentis*' for parental permission, by granting consent for the research *on behalf* of the child and the parent within the institution. However, wherever possible you should gain informed consent from the children themselves. The NCB (2003: 3) notes that 'It should not be assumed that the approval of a head teacher or unit manager for the research to take place equates to the consent of individual children'. Complete disclosure of all relevant information should *always* be given to children and young people, and their informed consent sought as well as the gatekeeper's. The institution may allow a researcher to give permission forms to the children to pass on to their parents, such as the letter below.

Example of letter seeking permission from the parents/guardians

---

Smiletown Nursery, Uptown.

Tuesday 23 October 2011

Dear Parent,

We have an authorised student, Helen Jones, working with us from Uptown College who wishes to carry out small-scale research with the children. She is looking at how Smiletown promotes the emotional development of the children. Such research will be valuable for the Nursery since it is good to get another perspective on what we do here with the children.

As part of Helen's research she wishes to consult with the children about what they like and dislike here; read stories with the children and do play improvisations; and carry out drawings and paintings.

Please read this letter with your child and discuss any questions that they may have. If you are happy for your child to participate in this research please sign and return the slip below.

Yours sincerely,
Joan Smith

I am happy for my child .... to participate in the research outlined above.
Signed Parent/Guardian ....

Case study

Helen's research was concerned with how a nursery can promote children's emotional development as required in the Early Years Foundation Stage (DCSF, 2008). Helen chose Smiletown Nursery for her research because it had recently been designated as a centre of excellence and was therefore more amenable to research. She initially wrote to the nursery manager, identifying herself, the research's aims and seeking permission to do the research at Smiletown Nursery (see permission letter, p.60). The manager took the request to a subsequent staff meeting and all the staff agreed that Helen could carry out the research. The staff suggested that the manager should write a letter to the parents outlining the research and that if the parents agreed they should sign and return the agreement slip at the bottom of the letter – see letter for parents, p.57. About half the parents responded positively to the letter and returned the agreement slip.

Helen phoned the manager to arrange a meeting to discuss further the research and to listen to the manager's suggestions for her research. It was agreed that Helen could visit the nursery for one day a week over a period of five weeks.

Together with the nursery staff, Helen explained to those children whose parents had agreed that they could participate in the research, that she had come to the nursery to find out what the children liked and disliked at the nursery. This would help the nursery to become an even friendlier place. Some of the children said they knew about the project because their mums and dads had told them it was 'okay' to do it. Helen asked the children what activities the children would like to do with her that would help her to understand more about the nursery. One child suggested that they could tell her about the things they liked and disliked and another suggested that they do drawings for Helen. Helen said she would do both those things with the children. One child wanted to know if Helen would get more toys for the nursery. Subsequently, Helen and a member of staff worked with this child in a group looking through children's toy catalogues to discuss what sort of toys the children wanted to buy.

The children were told that *today* Helen was going to read the 'Blue Kangaroo' and the children could then re-make the story using special finger puppets. Three children elected to work with Helen. Helen explained to these children that she would be using a tape recorder and showed the children how it worked and that they could turn it off at any time if they wished. The children had fun recording their voices and playing with the tape recorder. Helen explained that the tape was just for her to listen to but that she may have to tell the staff about any 'difficult things' that the children told her. The children said that this was okay.

Upon her return visit the following week Helen asked these three children if they wished to do a painting activity with her. Jane and Isabelle said 'no' because today they wanted to play outside with their friends. Jane and Isabelle clearly stated their preference and, although disappointed, Helen respected the girls' decision to withdraw from the research activity for the day. Different children wanted to join in the painting activity with Helen. On a subsequent occasion Jane and Isabelle agreed to participate in the research.

At the end of the research Helen gave the nursery staff a small booklet of her findings. This booklet had been carefully discussed with her supervisor since such a feedback document needs to be sensitively written. Helen also verbally shared the main findings of her research with the children. Helen listened carefully to the staff's and children's comments about her findings. She wanted to check that her interpretations of what she had seen and heard were acceptable to the children and the staff. As a thank-you present to the whole nursery Helen bought a big drum for the children to play with. She also made individual thank-you cards on her computer for the children and the staff who had participated in the research. She gave the nursery manager a box of chocolates.

Helen was aware that not all the children would have understood what she had told the children. She explained individually to the bilingual children what her research was about. Such individual explanation is critically important for some children. Helen made no assumptions about the children's participation and for each different research activity and experience their informed consent was renegotiated. Helen listened respectfully to the children's ideas about buying more toys for the nursery and with the agreement of the nursery staff asked the children what they wanted to buy from the catalogues. The children chose more musical instruments. This process helped the children to see that Helen took their suggestions seriously.

Gatekeepers' permission letter

A permission letter should be sent or given to the gatekeepers. If you are a student at a college or university, the permission letter should be printed on letter-headed paper with the institution's details. The gatekeepers and participants are entitled to know who is conducting the research and where they can be contacted. The permission letter should contain the following information.

- Identity of the researcher
  - The name(s) of the researcher.
  - An address and other contact details at which he or she can be contacted.
  - Where appropriate, the name of the organisation under whose auspices the research is being conducted.
- Information about the research
  - What the research questions are.

- What research techniques you will be using to collect your evidence.

- What potential benefits might arise from the research for the institution.

- Expectations about the participants' contribution

  - What tasks the participants will do.

  - How much of their time this is likely to take.

- Confidentiality and the security of evidence and data collected

  - What evidence will you be seeking to collect?

  - What will you do with that evidence when you have collected it?

  - Where and for how long will you keep it?

  - Who will see your research report?

  - How will you keep the information confidential?

Example of a letter seeking permission to carry out the research

This is an example of a letter which seeks permission to carry out research in a local nursery. The letter succinctly gives details of the researcher, explains the purposes of the research, what the research participants are expected to do, the confidentiality of the research and any possible benefits the nursery can expect from the research.

The Uptown University College,
Uptown Road,
Uptown.
Monday 27th September 2011

Dear Joan Smith, Manager of Smiletown Nursery,

My name is Helen Jones and I am in my final year at Uptown University College studying for my BA/BSc in Early Childhood Studies. As a prerequisite for the course I have had my Criminal Record Bureau (CRB) clearance. As part of my final year course I have to carry out and write up a small-scale piece of research totalling 6000 words. Smiletown nursery has been recommended since it is a Centre of Excellence. My research topic is concerned with the ways in which nurseries promote the emotional development of children.

My research questions are focused upon the diverse ways that nurseries understand and implement the emotional development of children. To collect information for my topic I would like to make some observations of your nursery and interview

---

yourself and other members of staff that you can recommend. The interviews would take approximately half an hour each. I would also hope to work with the children using stories, puppets, drawings and paintings. I will provide all paper, books and colouring materials. I would hope to be able to look at your policies too.

I will keep you informed of how the research is going throughout the project and give you a copy of my findings upon completion of the project. I would hope that the project would be of value to your institution in highlighting the ways in which Smiletown encourages the emotional development of children.

My Independent Study will be read by the University College tutors. The research will be kept confidential through anonymising the name of your institution and the research participants. I appreciate your time in reading this letter and will contact you by phone shortly to see if it is possible to meet with you to discuss the research further in your institution. If you wish to get in contact with me at any time my mobile number is 08978 456372 and my email is pj2@uptown.ac.uk.

Yours sincerely,
Helen Jones

I confirm that the above is a final year Early Childhood Studies student undertaking an Independent Study as part of her assessment. The student is bound by the Ethical Guidelines for all Uptown research which can be found at www.uptown/ethics.ac.uk. The research project plan has been passed by the Research Ethics Committee.

Yours sincerely
Gary Hills

Gary Hills, Early Childhood Studies Programme Director
Tel: 0188 56662. Email: GaryHills@Uptown
Department of Childhood Studies, Faculty of Education.

Researchers do not have a right to carry out their research in any institution that they wish. Remember that the gatekeepers of the institution are doing you a favour by allowing you access to carry out your research. They are potentially making themselves vulnerable by allowing the research to take place, since they have no absolute guarantee, other than your word, of what you will do with the information and evidence you collect from the institution. Access to institutions has to be carefully and sensitively carried out.

Permission to carry out your research in an institution needs to be sought at an early stage. Institutions may refuse access for a variety of reasons, including, for example, being too busy and the area you wish to investigate being too sensitive for the institution. Institutions are increasingly under inspection and surveillance from a variety of agencies, such as OFSTED, and may regard your research as yet another potentially threatening and unwelcome intrusion into their daily lives. If an institution refuses you permission, for whatever reason, you will have to locate another institution or carry out your research in a different way. Equally, an institution may welcome your research as a collaborative opportunity to learn with you. They may see that your research might have benefits for their institution in some way.

Even where you know the gatekeepers, namely the headteacher or manager, they need to be formally approached with your request to carry out some research in the institution. Thus you may already work in an institution in which you wish to carry out your research or you may have a relative who works in an appropriate institution or your child attends an institution in which you wish to carry out research. In these cases you have some connection with the gatekeepers of the institution and your task of gaining access is made all the easier. However, you should still make a formal request to carry out your research.

If the manager/headteacher grants you permission to carry out research, remember that they have the right to end your research in the institution at any time. Access is not a once and for all event but is something that needs continual negotiation. Remember, therefore, to dress appropriately and to be polite at all times to all the participants. If you have made arrangements to make observations on a particular morning, make sure you do so. Nurseries and schools are busy places and will not look kindly on researchers who do not keep their appointments. The trust in the relationship between you and the participants needs to be kept at all costs.

'Feedback' and closure of the research

It is ethically important to 'feed back' what you have learnt from the research participants. Feeding back some of your findings to the children and staff demonstrates how their views have been listened to and acknowledged by the researcher. Such feedback needs to be carefully discussed with your supervisor prior to handing it over to the institution. Since you are a first-time researcher and your research is a small-scale study, you are probably in no position to be publicly critical of an institution. It is best not to pass judgement on the evidence that you have been provided by the institution unless specifically asked to do so. This is part of your ethical responsibilities as a researcher. If asked, you can simply ask questions that the institution might want to investigate further.

Feeding back to the institution is a good opportunity to say thank you to all the staff and children for participating in the research. It is generous to give a thank-you card and perhaps a small present. You never know when you might go back to the institution! Saying thank you is important because it marks the end of the research. It is important for the children and staff to know that you have finished the research and are leaving. Sometimes a researcher builds up a good relationship with the children who must know that this relationship is going to end. Equally, this is the case with some researchers who become attached to the institution and the children.

Case study

After spending several weeks in a Year 2 class on her research project, Pam became close to the children. One child in particular had disclosed information which Pam found hard to accept. John had told Pam that both his parents had died in a car crash.

This really upset me and it took me a long time to find closure after I had carried out my project with John and his friends. I became very close to the children and knew a lot about them. John was so strong and resilient – I was in awe of his personal strength in a very difficult situation. It was hard for me to say goodbye to them at the end of the project.

The research process in the early childhood institution needs to be marked with closure, both for the benefit of the participants and the researcher.

Ethical dilemmas are hard to resolve

The identities and sets of relationships within your study will be unique. Thus, the ethical principles and dilemmas that you discuss will also be unique, set within the particular context of your study. The following case study shows how ethical issues are dependent upon their context and the research questions.

In the case study a mother initially decided to carry out some research with her son's drawings. Upon reflection, however, she was undecided as to whether or not it was ethically appropriate. Consider the following question as you read the example: what would you do in this mother/researcher's situation?

Since ethical dilemmas such as that below are often complex and unresolved, it is important to reflect *continuously* upon the ethical issues throughout the research.

There is a continual need for researchers to reflect on what they are doing and why they are doing it at every step of the research process. As part of this process researchers should also be reflexive about how their presence affects the research process (see Chapter 7).

📂 Case study

A mother/researcher had decided to carry out a project on children's understandings of their ethnic identities. The researcher's son was of mixed heritage and as part of the evidence collection for her project she initially decided to use her 4-year-old son's drawings. These drawings and the associated conversations pointed towards the fact that the boy had a sophisticated understanding of his complex identities. For example, the boy had curly hair but in his drawings he would sometimes draw himself with straight hair and sometimes with curly hair. His mother noted how this change in his hairstyle was dependent upon the context of the drawing. When his drawings showed him with white boys with straight hair, he chose to draw himself with straight hair. When his drawings showed him with other mixed heritage children he drew himself with curly hair. These drawings were positively interpreted by the mother/researcher as her son's attempt to make sense of his dual identity – of being both white and black. For the mother/researcher these drawings showed how observant and sensitive her son was of his dual heritage. She asked her son if she could put the pictures in her research project where they would be seen by her college. Her son agreed.

As the mother/researcher was finishing her research project and was ready to hand it in to the college she reflected upon the context in which her son had created the drawings. The drawings were made in the privacy of his home on the kitchen table with his mum. She reflected upon how the knowledge her son had co-produced with her was of a private, confidential and sensitive nature. She questioned whether her son would want such private knowledge to be read and possibly discussed at college. She was aware that the town they lived in was quite small and that therefore despite anonymising the drawings it would be possible to work out whose they were. She reflected upon how, as his mother, her son would tell and show her aspects of his life which he might not tell another person, such as his teacher. She was concerned that she did not want to exploit in any way aspects of her private mother/son relationship for her professional gain as a researcher. She was anxious that as her son got older he might interpret the research as being exploitative of an intimate relationship.

Ethical checklist

Access

- Written letter to gatekeepers, for example, nursery manager, headteacher, outlining the research aims and methods. This may be passed to other members of staff and/or discussed in a staff meeting. It may also be raised at a governors' meeting for their approval.
- Written letter to children's parents outlining the research and that the institution has granted you permission. Such a letter may include a tear-off slip for their signature.

Informed consent

- With young children continuous verbal negotiation.
- With older children a written leaflet and continuous verbal negotiation explaining the purposes of the research and what the children are expected to do.
- Show staff/practitioners/teachers a copy of the letter to the headteacher/nursery manager seeking permission for the research. Verbally gain informed consent by reminding research participants of the research's aims, what you will do with the information collected, confidentiality and that they do not have to participate if they choose not to.

Summary 🔲

This chapter has:

- discussed the legal and social importance of listening to children's voices
- demonstrated the researcher's ethical responsibilities concerning informed consent, confidentiality and child protection
- reflected upon the complexity associated with gaining informed consent with young children and ways in which to tell children about the research
- shown how ethical dilemmas are rarely resolved but need to be reflected upon by the researcher
- discussed the importance of providing feedback to the research participants and providing closure for the research.

Recommended reading

Alderson, P. (2008) *Young Children's Rights: Exploring Beliefs, Principles and Practice*, 2nd edn. London: Jessica Kingsley.
This book gives an authoritative guide to the critical issues of children and human rights. It is a very useful text for practitioners since it directly addresses their context. The book is packed full of stimulating and provocative case studies which are useful to think about in the context of your research project.

Coady, M. (2010) 'Ethics in early childhood research', in G. MacNaughton, S. Rolfe and I. Siraj-Blatchford (2010) *Doing Early Childhood Research*, 2nd edn. Maidenhead: Open University Press.
This chapter provides a detailed and thorough overview of the history of ethics in early childhood research. The chapter includes insightful discussion on the cultural issues in ethical research as well as practical advice on how to submit your proposal to the ethics committee.

4

Designing your research

Learning objectives

This chapter will help you to:

- begin to design and plan your research
- reflect upon the connection between your research questions and the methodology of your study
- understand the quantitative and qualitative research approaches
- reflect upon the sample for your study
- understand the importance of triangulated research to validate your findings
- become familiar with action research, case studies and surveys.

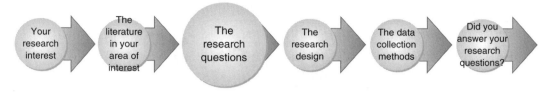

Figure 4.1   The relationship between research questions and research design

What is research design?

Research design is concerned with your research methodology, approach and data collection methods and the subsequent analysis of your data. The research design connects your research questions to your research data (See Figure 4.1).

Your experience, interests and reading will inform your research questions. Remember, the more specific your research questions the more focused your research will be. The way in which you have written your research questions will determine your research design. If you have asked open-ended type research questions then your research design will tend to follow the qualitative approach. For example, the following research questions lend themselves towards a qualitative research design and approach.

- Why and how do children in a nursery use their outdoor environment?
- To what extent do early childhood practitioners believe in a play-based approach to learning?
- What do early childhood practitioners understand by the term professional?
- How does a nursery communicate with the parents and carers?

The above four questions can be successfully answered using a qualitative design and approach, whereas the following four questions tend to lend themselves towards a quantitative design and approach.

- How frequently do children use the outdoor environment?
- What is the relationship between the qualifications of nursery staff and outcomes for children?
- Do children who frequently play together show higher language development?
- Does organic food without sugar result in better children's behaviour?

Table 4.1   Differences between the qualitative and quantitative research approaches

Qualitative research approach	Quantitative research approach
Does not attempt generalisations	Attempts to generalise from findings
Seeks multiple truths with a variety of people's understandings and perspectives	Seeks a particular truth
Acknowledges and works with researcher subjectivity and bias	Attempts researcher objectivity
Process orientated	Outcome orientated
Assumes a dynamic reality	Assumes a stable reality
Validity of findings are specific, local and contextual	Validity of findings dependent upon their research replication by another researcher doing the same project

In this way it can be seen that the research questions themselves determine the research approach that is used.

Two research approaches

The quantitative and qualitative research approaches are two ways of understanding the world and human behaviour within it. Your research questions will determine the research approach which you choose to work with (Clough and Nutbrown, 2007). It is important to understand what the qualitative research approach is, where it has come from and why it differs from the quantitative research approach (Table 4.1). By understanding the different research approaches you will be better able to plan and carry through your research project. Quantitative or positivist researchers are usually associated with quantitative methods and qualitative or interpretive researchers with qualitative methods. However, quantitative and qualitative researchers can use a mixture of both qualitative and quantitative research methods.

A useful analogy for these two approaches of quantitative and qualitative research is that of photography. When taking pictures the quantitative researcher tends to take the wide-angled, broad sweep and panoramic photographs. These show the whole broad scope of the situation without much detail. The qualitative researcher, on the other hand, tends to take the close-up, detailed photographs. These show the fine detail and complex interactions going on. Both are useful in that we get to see different perspectives of the same thing. Such different perspectives are also useful in ensuring your study has triangulation.

Quantitative research

Quantitative research is the traditional scientific way of seeing the world (Punch, 2009). Quantitative researchers believe that 'the truth is out there' waiting to be discovered and tend to believe that the world is logical and obeys rational scientific laws such as the 'cause and effect' principle. It is argued that human interactions are part of the scientific laws of nature and can thus be measured and quantified in the same way as atoms and chemicals. Quantitative researchers may state a hypothesis or an assumption which they then set out to prove as either true or false. They tend to use experiments and large sample sizes in order to generalise from their findings.

For quantitative researchers, if the results of a specific research project are valid, they can be replicated, or copied, by another researcher when the project is repeated (Punch, 2009). Thus validity for quantitative researchers is not influenced by the researcher him/herself and anybody else should be able to carry out the same research and get the same results.

Qualitative research

Within the qualitative approach it is understood that the social world is created by our shared cultural understandings of situations (Punch, 2009). Qualitative research is based in a belief that we continually create and construct our social world by negotiating with others the *meanings* of our actions. Qualitative researchers are interested in the complexity and diversity of human interactions. For qualitative researchers, people and organisations tend to be contradictory and sometimes irrational. Within an early childhood setting the *interpretation* of events by the researcher, the children, the parents and nursery workers are all equally important. For the qualitative researcher these multiple understandings are all equally important and the range of interpretations gives the research validity. Qualitative researchers tend not to generalise from their research and have smaller sample sizes than in quantitative research. For the qualitative researcher, validity is dependent upon accurately representing the voices and experiences of the research participants. The authenticity of the research participants' responses can be demonstrated by cross-checking or triangulating their responses with other people. Through this process of data triangulation it is possible to see if the participants' responses are consistent.

Sampling within your project

It is clearly impossible for you to study all children or all early childhood settings. So researchers sample or select just a handful of children or early childhood settings to study. It is how this small selection is chosen that is known within research as sampling. It is important within your research project to state how your sample was chosen. Whether your research is qualitative or quantitative it is important to be clear on how and why you have sampled or selected the early childhood setting(s) or child(ren), or whatever it is that you are studying. If you have sampled a particular early childhood setting case study then you must explain how and why you have selected that particular setting. Clear explanation of your sampling strategy enhances the validity of your research design.

Quantitative researchers tend to attempt a representative sample. They do this because they wish to generalise their findings from the sample that they have selected to the wider population. They do this through probability sampling which is based upon a random selection. For example, if an early childhood researcher were surveying the amount of time that children played outdoors within nurseries, then they might randomly sample 10 nurseries from within a city to study. Each nursery would have an equal probability of being chosen. It would be claimed that these 10 nurseries would be a representative sample of all the city's nurseries. From these 10 randomly selected nurseries a quantitative researcher would attempt to make generalisations from their findings for all nurseries within the city. This representative sampling would contribute to the research design's validity.

However, qualitative researchers, on the other hand, would rarely use such random sampling. Qualitative early childhood researchers tend to use some sort of deliberate sampling such as purposive sampling. Purposive sampling is where the researcher deliberately chooses to sample particular setting(s) or child(ren) to study. This is because that particular setting or child may provide a good example of what the researcher is investigating. Thus if a researcher was investigating the benefits of outdoor play and learning they may purposively sample a nursery which has very good outdoor facilities. They may contrast this with a nursery that has poorly developed outdoor provision. If a researcher were investigating practitioners' beliefs about child-centred learning they might purposively sample Montessori nursery teachers' beliefs (which are known to be child centred) with those of teachers in a more formal Reception class in a primary school. In both these examples the researcher has deliberately or purposively sampled settings that will help them to answer their research questions.

In addition to the purposive sampling above, you may have sampled your setting because you have a connection with it. This is known as convenience sampling. You may work there or have worked there in the past or your friend works there and you therefore have good access to the setting and feel comfortable carrying out your research there. It is therefore convenient for you to do your research in that setting. However, even within this convenience sample setting, you will have to sample the practitioners and children that you study. These may be randomly sampled, as above, for example you may choose every third child on the register to observe or every third teacher alphabetically. Thus you can make representative samples within conveniently sampled settings.

Triangulation and validity

Triangulation is the research practice of comparing and combining different sources of evidence in order to reach a better understanding of the research topic. Triangulation gives qualitative research validity and makes the findings more convincing (Mukherji and Albon, 2009). Triangulation involves the researcher collecting a range of evidence by using a variety of research methods. Triangulation gives the researcher the opportunity to check out their evidence from a range of sources. It is important to try to get different perspectives. For example, if you were interested in a teacher's practice it would be insufficient to simply ask them about their practice in an interview. You would also need to observe what they do and possibly ask for the children's perspectives on their teacher too. In this manner you would be relying upon three sources of evidence:

* what the teacher told you in the interview
* your observations of what the teacher actually does
* the children's perspectives on their teacher's practice.

Gail's study on work and play in the Foundation Stage involved listening to the perspectives of the children, the teachers and the parents. Gail made observations of what was happening in the class and followed this up with interviews with the teachers and the children. She also questionnaired the parents about their views on work and play in the Reception class (see Figure 4.2).

Lucy's study on domestic violence involved a large questionnaire sample as well as interviews with a range of professionals. The interviews and questionnaires provided different perspectives from different professions thus providing Lucy's study with triangulation (see Figure 4.3).

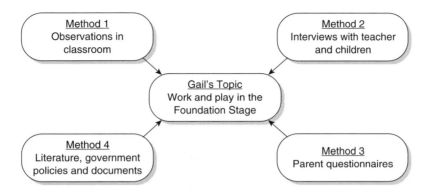

Figure 4.2   Gail's methodological triangulation

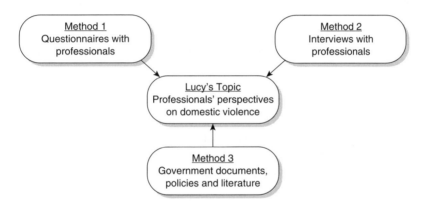

Figure 4.3   Lucy's methodological triangulation

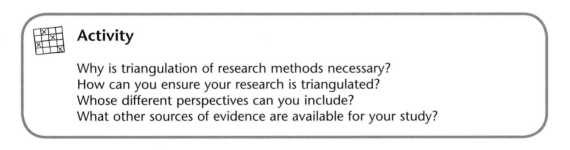

The quantitative and qualitative approaches: an example

Suppose two early childhood researchers are looking into the topic of television cartoon violence and its relationship with children. In the following

Table 4.2   Research topic: television violence

Quantitative approach	Qualitative approach
Hypothesis stated	Series of open-ended questions
Connection between two variables assumed	No assumptions made
Experiment devised with randomly sampled test and control groups	Purposively sampled case study described
Children perceived as research objects to be monitored and observed	Children perceived as thinking active people whose understandings are paramount
Large representative sample size selected	Representative sample not important, but rich contextualisation is important
Complexity of topic minimised to allow for generalisations to be made	Complexity and diversity of children's understandings sought. No generalisations to be made
Ethical issues should be central	Ethical issues inform the research process throughout from planning to approaches to techniques
Researcher bias ignored	Researcher bias discussed
Concepts and themes and techniques, analysis and interpretation established prior to the research being carried out	Concepts and themes and techniques, analysis and interpretation emerge as the research progresses

example the first study belongs within the quantitative approach and the second study within the qualitative approach. The differences between the two approaches (Table 4.2) are deliberately accentuated for the purposes of understanding each.

The researchers wish to understand more about violence on television and if this imagined violence has any detrimental effect upon children's behaviour.

Television cartoon violence: the quantitative approach

The hypothesis:

Children who watch violent and aggressive television cartoons will role-play aggressively.

A hypothesis has been stated that there is a causal connection between two variables. The two variables are aggressive television shows, on the one hand, and subsequent aggressive play, on the other. The hypothesis or statement suggests that there is a direct connection between these two variables. Within the quantitative approach the researcher will set out to test whether the hypothesis or the statement is either true or false.

The researcher following the quantitative approach will devise detailed procedures before beginning the project. The project may devise an experiment possibly along the following lines. A large sample size of representative children will be located. The children will be divided into two research groups: a group exposed to aggressive television cartoons and a control group whose television viewing is filtered out for violence. Direct comparisons will be made between the experimental group and the control group of children. Other variables connected to potential violence will also be noted and removed from the experiment. The two groups of children's role-play activities will be monitored subsequently. The data collected will be statistically analysed and interpreted and the hypothesis will be either proved correct or incorrect.

Television cartoon violence: the qualitative approach

Overall research study questions:

- What do children understand by the word 'violence'?
- Do they perceive certain television shows as being violent?
- How do children understand and make sense of these violent television shows in their games?

This time the same research topic has been phrased as three open-ended questions. The questions are phrased in such a way that the children's diverse perceptions and understandings of 'violence', television and role play are central to the research. The children are understood as actively engaged participants whose understandings and perceptions of the research topic frames the research as it progresses.

Unlike the quantitative research there is no assumption made about a connection between 'violent' television and subsequent children's role play. The questions are open, tentative and do not predict outcomes or causal connections. The first question acknowledges that the notion of violence on television is itself open to different interpretations. What may be perceived by the researcher as 'violent' may not be seen as such by the children. This opening question problematises the whole notion of the project and will lead to greater complexity and understanding of the topic.

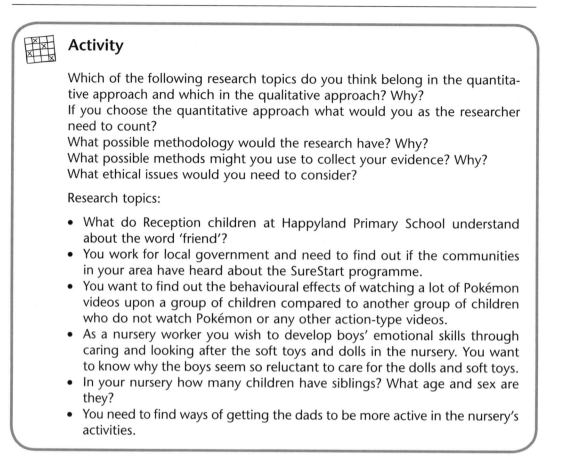

Activity

Which of the following research topics do you think belong in the quantitative approach and which in the qualitative approach? Why?
If you choose the quantitative approach what would you as the researcher need to count?
What possible methodology would the research have? Why?
What possible methods might you use to collect your evidence? Why?
What ethical issues would you need to consider?

Research topics:

- What do Reception children at Happyland Primary School understand about the word 'friend'?
- You work for local government and need to find out if the communities in your area have heard about the SureStart programme.
- You want to find out the behavioural effects of watching a lot of Pokémon videos upon a group of children compared to another group of children who do not watch Pokémon or any other action-type videos.
- As a nursery worker you wish to develop boys' emotional skills through caring and looking after the soft toys and dolls in the nursery. You want to know why the boys seem so reluctant to care for the dolls and soft toys.
- In your nursery how many children have siblings? What age and sex are they?
- You need to find ways of getting the dads to be more active in the nursery's activities.

Action research

At the heart of this research strategy is the notion of instigating change in the institution. Such change might be in the form of practice, policy and/or culture within an institution (MacNaughton and Hughes, 2008). Action research is concerned with practically changing an issue within the working environment to improve the researcher's and their colleagues' knowledge and practice. Consequently, action research is a fairly complex and time-consuming approach to research involving the researcher's colleagues too. Action research is sometimes known as the 'practitioner as researcher' approach because the researcher and the practitioner is the same person. Action research rejects the concept of a two-stage process in which research is carried out first by researchers and then, in a separate second stage, the knowledge generated from the research is applied by practitioners. Instead, the two processes of action and research are integrated.

Action research is a collaborative strategy and often involves the participants of the research such as the nursery workers, parents and children in planning and carrying out the research with the researcher. Action research is thus democratic and inclusive. For small-scale first-time researchers the nature of change in their practice and institution is likely to be small.

Action research example

Janet wanted to ensure that the children's centre was inclusive. So they used *The Index for Inclusion* (Booth and Ainscow, 2004). The Index encourages all stakeholders in the children's centre to ask a series of questions concerning their practice, policies and culture. Janet arranged a series of meetings with all her staff about inclusion and what her colleagues thought it meant and whether or not they believed their institution and practices were inclusive. Such discussions in themselves proved to be hugely informative for the staff. In addition, from these discussions the staff identified three main issues they wished to investigate further:

- Were all the nursery's diverse range of children participating in all the activities the nursery provided?

- What barriers prevented some children from participating in certain activities?

- What resources were needed to ensure that participation became a reality for all children?

The staff made observations on all the children within their care over a two-month period. They then met again and discussed their findings. Several members of staff noted that the boys and girls did not play together on the 'wheelie toys' and construction activities. It was also noted that the children with physical difficulties were not using the wheelie toys. The staff agreed to discuss with the children whether and how girls and boys could play with wheelie toys and construction equipment together. What were the children's opinions of this? What were the children's suggestions? They agreed to buy specialised wheelie toys for the children with physical difficulties. They then put this action plan into practice and met again in another two weeks to see if this had improved their practice.

It was found that the children were more aware that boys and girls should be playing together in these activities. There were still, however, problems and it was decided to suggest to the children 'girl only' sessions for short periods of time and see what the children thought of this and how this would work out (MacNaughton, 2000). The staff worked on this idea for two weeks and then met to discuss their reflections.

The specialised wheelies had made a big difference for the children with physical difficulties and the staff decided to buy further specialised play equipment for children. It was noted that all the children enjoyed using the specialised equipment too.

In the above example it can be seen how action research develops and builds upon its findings and continues to ask further questions. Action research is thus a cyclical and long-term process rather than a 'one-off' piece of research. Ideally, it should involve all stakeholders in the research process throughout.

Activity: Design your own practitioner research

Collaboratively think of an issue/problem within your early years institution. Draw an action research cycle involving all the issues on big sheets of paper for display.

Does your proposed action research address a practical problem?
How was the problem identified?
Who will be involved with the research? Why?
Is the action research part of a continuous cycle of development, rather than a one-off project?
Is there a clear view of how the research findings will feed back directly into practice?

Action research belongs to you

Sometimes action research is referred to as 'practitioner research' because *you*, the practitioner, are at the centre of the research – hence the name 'practitioner research'. One of the great things about doing *your* early years reflective practice research project is that *you* become the centre of *your* project. Action research is *insider* research. *You* are the insider and hence the central aspect of the project! As with all research, action research involves a systematic enquiry of asking questions, collecting evidence, and analysing and evaluating the findings supported by a range of evidence.

Traditional research projects employ outsiders who are early years 'experts'. These 'experts' might be senior managers, lecturers, council policy writers, or advisors. They might come to your early years setting with *their* agendas, ideas and questions they wish to investigate. The research questions and agendas may have been written elsewhere and may or may not have relevance for you and your early years setting. These 'experts' might come to your early years setting, observe, make comments and recommendations and then disappear. In this traditional research project you become a participant in somebody else's research project. The exciting thing about action research is that you develop unique knowledge about yourself and your early years setting.

The early years reflective action research cycle

In the early years reflective action research cycle, illustrated in Figure 4.4, the practitioner (you!) has identified an issue in your practice that you wish to

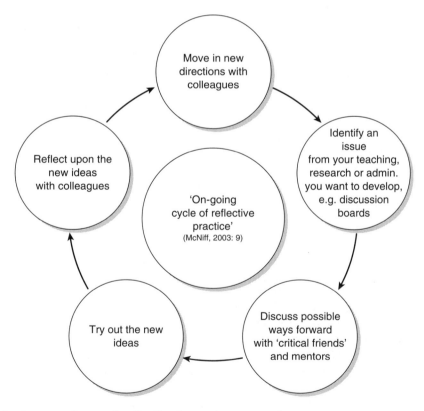

Figure 4.4   An on-going cycle of reflective action research

investigate further. You discuss this issue with your friends and read around the issue. You then try out a new way of doing things, reflect on what was happening and then, in the light of your reflections, try a new way. The process is on-going because when you have discovered a new way of doing things that point itself raises new questions that you can investigate.

Simon's story of reflective action research

In the following case study you can see that Simon's work as an Early Years Foundation Stage teacher, was driven by his values and principles concerning children's creativity.

Case study

Simon's story

I work in the Early Years Foundation Stage in a large urban primary school. I am one of two Reception class teachers. I have been teaching this age group for the past five years and am concerned that less and less time is spent upon creative activities with the children. This is frustrating because when I was at college we read lots of literature about how children's creativity needs to be encouraged for their happiness and well-being. Unfortunately, there is such pressure from the rest of the school for the children to leave the EYFS with high standards in numeracy and literacy that there is little time for anything else! This is the problem that I identified as needing to be further explored in a reflective action research project. I framed my reflective research project around the following central research question: 'To what extent is there a lack of creativity in the Early Years Foundation Stage in my Primary School?'

I organised focus group discussions with EYFS colleagues in this school and another one a mile or so away about this issue. This was very interesting and we decided to keep a timetable and to calculate exactly how much time we spent on creative work with the children each week. The discussions and the timetables provided evidence that colleagues were frustrated by the lack of time allocated to creativity in the EYFS, especially in the Reception classes. I wrote all this up as a reflective practice research project but I wanted to do more. How could I change this situation so that I was able to work in line with my beliefs and values about young children's learning? I was very lucky as at that time there were some grants made available for teachers to make study tours to other countries. I chose Denmark as I knew that there was a lot of creativity in schools there. Once there I talked to many early

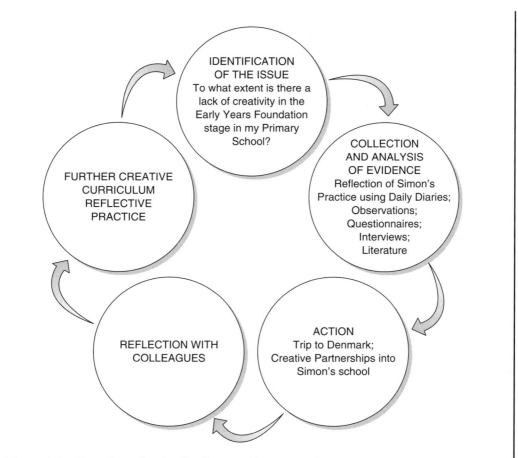

Figure 4.5   Simon's cycle of reflective practice research

years teachers who were able to spend far more time working creatively with children. In the Danish primary school I experienced levels of creativity amongst the children unseen in my school in Bristol. Upon my return I shared my experiences with the whole staff. Some colleagues, including the headteacher, were very enthusiastic to develop the ideas. With the support of the headteacher, I set about a further project to encourage creativity amongst staff and children in Foundation Stage. After much discussion together, we decided to work with an 'Artist in Residence' in the school. The artist and subsequent reflective practice dialogue has further transformed the EYFS staff's understandings and beliefs concerning children's creativity and learning. The whole action research project has reinvigorated my working life and given it added meaning and purpose!

As a consequence of this action research, Simon has generated theory about children's creativity, developing confidence and improved performance in the classroom. Simon has plenty of evidence to support his beliefs that creativity is important for children's well-being and classroom performance. Simon knows what he is doing and why he is doing it. He can justify his practice with his locally produced knowledge. This situated knowledge is supported by literature. His reflective practice project is in line with his values and principles about how young children learn best. This action research project has enthused and motivated his work as an Early Years Foundation Stage teacher.

Case studies

Case studies tend to have a narrowly defined focus on an individual, a family or one or two early childhood institutions. 'The case study method is most likely to be appropriate for "how" and "why" questions' (Yin, 2009: 27) and these questions are asked of a particular setting(s). Case studies are small and the boundaries and parameters of the research project are fairly clear and, hence, the researcher can concentrate all their time and effort focusing upon a narrow and clearly defined situation. Case studies are good for drawing out the detail and complexity of intricate social relationships within an institution. Case studies need to be richly contextualised with plenty of 'thick' detailed description to give the reader a good sense and feel for the institution under investigation. It is important to note that generalisations concerning the research topic cannot be made from a case study.

The first example below is that of a *single* case study. This is known as an 'intrinsic' case study and can be used to study a unique or typical case (Yin, 2009: 48). The second example below is that of a *multiple* case study design. 'The evidence from multiple cases is often considered more compelling and the overall study is therefore regarded as being more robust' (Yin, 2009: 53). For the beginner researcher, the multiple case study can be comparing and contrasting two case study contexts that are similar but are representative of the difference being studied. The second case study lends itself to being comparative because both the EYP and the teacher work with the same age group on Early Years Foundation Stage and are both comparable women working in the same geographical area. Thus they are *comparative* case studies.

Example of a single case study

Sarah's research topic was concerned with the relationship between gender and friendships amongst a sample of ten 6-year-old children (five boys and five girls). She chose this sample of children because she knew that these children had very strong relationships based upon family friendships and time spent together at nursery. Thus the children were representative of a typical case.

Sarah's specific research questions were:

- How do young children understand friendship?

- How do young children understand gender?

- Is there a relationship between gender and friendship amongst young children? If so, why is this?

Sarah's questions were centrally concerned with the subtleties and intricacies of friendship amongst young children. She wanted to find out if there was a relationship between young children's gender and their friendship. To answer such questions demanded the collection of delicate, sensitive and complex evidence from a small number of children. Hence, an in-depth case study is the ideal approach to answer Sarah's research questions.

Research techniques that Sarah included to answer her questions were group interviews, observations of children inside and outside the classroom, drawings by the children of their friendships and the games they played together. Sarah also interviewed the teacher and the parents of the sample children. Such research techniques provided the level of complexity Sarah needed to answer her how and why questions.

Example of a multiple comparative case study

Tom, who was studying to become an Early Years Professional (EYP), was interested in comparing the working experiences of an EYP with those of a qualified early years teacher. He selected a private day nursery which employed an EYP to teach 3–4 year olds and compared this person's working experiences with those of a qualified teacher working in a nursery school teaching the same age group.

Both professionals were female and of approximately the same age and the settings were in the same district of the city drawing the same socio-economic mix of children.

Tom's research questions were:

- How do an EYP and a qualified teacher experience their daily working lives?

- What is similar and different about an EYP and an early years teacher's daily working life?

- Why is the EYP and the teacher's daily working life, both different and similar from one another?

As with all case studies, Tom used a wide range of data collection techniques in order to triangulate the data. He carried out a series of observations over time and several in-depth interviews with both the professionals individually and, on one occasion, together. He was also able to interview the headteacher of the nursery school and the manager of the private day nursery. Additionally, he compared and contrasted the policies and terms and conditions of employment between the EYP and the teacher.

Small-scale qualitative surveys

It is important to note that not all small-scale qualitative studies are case studies. Some small-scale qualitative research are small surveys. 'Even small populations – such as the parents and staff of a nursery – can be surveyed' (Siraj-Blatchford, 2010: 223). A small-scale qualitative survey usually utilises both questionnaires and structured interviews. Through the use of fixed interview questioning as found in structured interviews and questionnaires, all the respondents in the small survey are asked the same questions. Once the evidence has been collected, the researcher attempts to extract patterns and comparisons from the data. Surveys are particularly attractive for researchers who wish to statistically analyse their evidence. Surveys lend themselves to generating percentage points and graphs which clearly show the researcher's findings. Surveys are good at producing breadth of evidence but a downside is that they can consequently lack depth.

In the first example which follows, Lucy used a small-scale survey research design to answer her questions concerned with the professional perspectives of domestic violence. In the second example Hua Jong was interested in examining the partnership between teachers and parents in a pre-school in South China.

Small-scale survey example one

Lucy wanted to know the professional perspectives on domestic violence from a whole range of professions dealing with children: teachers, playgroup workers, social workers, domestic violence officers and family liaison officers. She was looking for evidence to analyse statistically and thus the small-scale survey strategy suited her purposes. Whilst gaining *breadth* of evidence from the survey of many different professions, Lucy lost the depth needed to answer the more complex and subtle issues within her research project. Thus, combined within the overall survey, Lucy carried out three in-depth interviews with a range of the professionals. These interviews helped to flesh out the complexity of issues raised by the 'bare bones' provided by the survey.

Small-scale survey example two

Hua Jong was interested in finding out more about partnerships between early childhood teachers and parents in a pre-school in South China. Hence she conducted a small-scale survey in one particular school. Initially, Hua carried out pilot interviews with two teachers and two parents. This helped her to establish the main issues and from these pilot interviews she wrote a questionnaire and a structured interview schedule with fixed questions that focused upon the parent–teacher partnership and relationship. Hua then piloted the questionnaires and the structured interviews with the two teachers and the two parents. After making all necessary amendments she randomly distributed the questionnaires. After agreement from the headteacher Hua selected every third teacher and every third parent from an alphabetical register. This process ensured random sampling, which added to the research's reliability. From the data collected, Hua was able to both quantitatively and qualitatively analyse the survey data and the structured questionnaire data.

Broad and deep research

Some early childhood studies achieve breadth and generalisability at the same time. Figure 4.6 has plotted onto it the different research projects discussed in this chapter. Lucy's survey is a broad and general study whilst her interviews will be specific and deep and, hence, are plotted in opposite corners of the diagram. Gail's and Sarah's case studies are specific but are also fairly broad in their questions. Janet's action research is also plotted in this cell because it involves a large number of people within a single institution. Different aspects of a study can be plotted in different cells according to their specificity and generalisability.

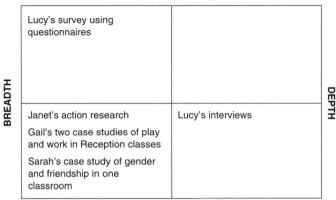

Figure 4.6 Research can be plotted along two axes: general/specific and breadth/depth (adapted from Clough and Nutbrown, 2007)

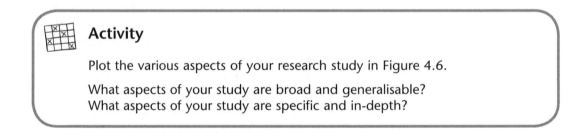

Activity

Plot the various aspects of your research study in Figure 4.6.

What aspects of your study are broad and generalisable?
What aspects of your study are specific and in-depth?

Justifying your methods

In your research you must justify and explain your research methods, and your choice of setting and research participants. This *justification* of your research methods shows you understand *why* you have used certain methods and not others (Clough and Nutbrown, 2007).

In your research you should be able to explain:

• what your overall research questions are

• what sort of, and how much, information you need to answer your research questions

- what field questions you need to ask to get this information

- *why* you have chosen a particular setting to research

- *why* you used certain methods and not others.

Whatever methods you decide to choose in order to answer your research questions, you must provide a rationale for those decisions. Providing a rationale and explanation for such research methods shows that you understand *why* you have done interviews rather than questionnaires and *why* you have interviewed practitioners but not children. For example, whether you decide to interview two early years students at great depth and length, or survey 50 early years students at random in the students' café, you must say *why* you made these choices. Of course, you may choose to do a handful of in-depth interviews *and* lots of questionnaires, but you must explain why you would do both and how your research would be improved by doing both. The key message is to *justify* whatever research methods you choose to do.

Sarah's overall research questions were concerned with the ways in which children's friendships are gendered. Specifically, her research questions centred upon children's understanding of the words 'friendships' and 'boys' and 'girls'. Sarah wanted to gain *insights* into the issue of friendships from the perspectives of the children themselves and was more concerned with issues of depth rather than breadth. At the heart of Sarah's research was a desire to *explore* the issue of childhood friendships rather than wanting to prove a hypothesis or statement about friendships. This complex topic was ideally suited to using interviews since interviews are able to elicit the sort of subtle, ambiguous and sometimes contradictory issues that arise with friendships. Sarah also wanted the perspective of the class teacher on the notions of childhood friendships and, hence, interviewed the teacher too. Rather than interviewing and questionnairing all 60 children in the year group, she opted for in-depth observations, interviews and drawings with 12 children and one interview with a teacher. Sarah noted subtle responses from the children when she interviewed them and was able to explore in depth some of the children's emotions, feelings and experiences around their friendships. Thus, interviewing was an appropriate method for Sarah to use because her overall research questions demanded insight into the children's perceptions. Using questionnaires, which would have been logistically difficult since not all the children could read and write, would not have elicited the subtle and contradictory evidence the research questions demanded.

Your research proposal

There is a notable relationship between the quality of a research proposal and the subsequent quality of the research itself. All research, whether large and complex and supported by grant money or relatively small research projects need to have a good clear and ethically sound research proposal. Your research proposal should clearly state: what it is that the research is trying to find out more about; why this research is worth doing; what will be learnt as a consequence of doing this research; and how you will go about collecting and analysing the data. In other words, the proposal describes what will be done. The research is only carried out after the research proposal has been approved. Writing a good research proposal involves considerable work.

The proposal is expected to demonstrate:

- what you are finding out more about

- that your research is worthwhile

- that you are familiar with the major theoretical ideas and recent research in the area

- that you have an understanding of a particular theoretical orientation in your research area

- that you can justify your methodological approach and data collecting methods

- that you have thought about the ethical issues.

The areas to be discussed in your research proposal may include the following (adapted from Punch, 2009: 330):

1 Title
2 Abstract
3 Introduction:

   Area and topic
   Background and context
   Statement of purpose – what you hope to learn more about
   Importance of the study – why your study is important

4 Research questions

5 The literature
6 Design and methods: strategy and design

   Sampling
   Data collection instruments and procedures
   Data analysis

7 Access and ethical considerations
8 References
9 Appendices, which may include timetable and costs.

Title and abstract

The proposed title and the abstract can be written *after* you have completed your proposal since you will have a clearer idea of the research through the process of writing the proposal. You will then be in a better position to write the abstract and think of a creative title.

Introduction

Within the proposal introduction you need to clearly show the research area and topic and write what the study proposes to find out more about. The introduction should also show how the study fits into existing knowledge in the topic area. In addition, your personal knowledge and experience form part of the context of the study and can be included in the introduction. You need to state why your research is timely and important to carry out. How will your research contribute to existing knowledge?

Research questions

These are important and have been discussed earlier in this chapter and in Chapter 2. The key to writing good research questions is to ensure that they are specific and achievable. Make sure that your questions are viable and feasible – in other words can you answer them within the given time?

The literature

The purpose of the literature review is to provide the background to your own study and to identify the key research in the area. You need to be able to demonstrate your understanding of research findings and issues related to your topic. Clearly the literature review in a proposal will not be completely comprehensive.

That will occur later in the study itself, but it must give an indication that you understand *how* your study fits in with the existing research and ideas in the area under investigation.

Design and methods

In this section you need to write about and justify the strategy that your study will adopt to answer the research questions. Explain why you are adopting a qualitative or quantitative research methodology. How does this methodology fit with your research questions? If set within the qualitative paradigm, will your research design be a case study or case studies, a small-scale survey, an ethnography, or will it be action research? Carefully explain why you have chosen a particular design and how this design will help to answer your research questions. Will you carry out a pilot study? If not, why? If a quantitative study, will your research have hypotheses and be an experiment measuring pre- and post-test variables? Whatever your research design you must *justify* your choices.

Sampling

In this section you must state what your sampling strategy will be and why. What is the size of your sample to be, how is it to be selected and why? Sampling is an important aspect of the validity of your project.

Data collection

What are the data collection methods that you will utilise? What methods are appropriate and feasible? How will you actually carry out the real data collection? Will your project use questionnaires and interviews and observations? If so, why?

Data analysis

Data analysis is an important section to include in your proposal. You need to demonstrate that you are familiar with the different analytic techniques and how you will use them. What computer software will you use?

Ethical issues

Ethical issues are dealt with in depth in the previous chapter. Your study should be ethically sound, that is you should gain the informed consent of all the participants at every step of the data collection process. You should clearly state how you intend to gain access to the participants and, if appropriate, the case study settings.

References

Finally, you need to include the list of references that you have used in the proposal.

The following common mistakes are made in proposal writing:

- A lack of the proper context to frame your research study
- Not accurately presenting the contributions and references of other researchers.
- Lack of focus on the research questions and not addressing the research questions.

Summary

This chapter has:

- provided an overview of the major differences between the quantitative and qualitative research approaches
- evaluated the role of sampling in your research design
- examined the issues of validity and triangulation
- discussed action research, case study research and surveys
- provided an overview for your research proposal.

Recommended reading

Mukherji, P. and Albon, D. (2009) *Research Methods in Early Childhood: An Introductory Guide*. London: Sage Publications.
This is a thorough methodological textbook which provides a good description of the whole early childhood research process. There are clear descriptions

of the different research paradigms, approaches and methods in early childhood.

MacNaughton, G. and Hughes, P. (2008) *Doing Action Research in Early Childhood Studies*. Buckingham: Open University Press.
The book introduces and evaluates different approaches to action research and explores how they can be applied in early childhood settings to create positive change and to improve practice. It is written in a user-friendly manner and illustrated with clear case studies.

5

Organising and writing up your research project

Learning objectives

This chapter will help you to:

- reflect upon the nature of critical writing
- understand the organisation of your writing
- be alerted to ways to write the literature review
- understand the dangers of plagiarism
- be aware of your and your supervisor's responsibilities.

You should try to read and write throughout the duration of your research project. The more you read the better your writing will become. Your thinking about a subject develops as you write, so the more you write, the clearer your understanding and ideas will be. A central aspect of academic writing is an argument.

Writing an academic argument and critical writing

People understand issues in different ways in early childhood studies and these differing viewpoints or ways of seeing an issue are known as arguments or propositions. An argument is a proposition or a way of thinking about an idea. The key to an argument is to try to persuade the reader of your ideas. For example, there is much debate as to why boys and girls seem to behave in different ways. An argument is that boys and girls have different genetic make-ups, leading to boys being interested in certain activities and toys whilst girls' genes lead them to different behaviour, toys and activities. These people subscribe to the 'nature' argument, believing that genes determine the behaviour of the sexes. Literature is then used and quoted to support this argument such as Maccoby (1996). In your study therefore you can state a proposition or argument and then cite literature sources.

The counterargument(s) now needs to be presented. This is the opposite argument to the original proposition. Key words with which to present a counterargument include 'however', 'but', and 'on the other hand'. For example, 'the "Nurture" proponents *on the other hand* believe that boys and girls are socialised in different ways from birth with self-fulfilling expectations of different behaviour and interests between the sexes' (MacNaughton, 2000). Then you must cite literature from this side of the argument to support these views. If *gender issues* are part of your study, your literature needs to show that you are aware of *both viewpoints* of nature and nurture. Your research project must engage with the nature/nurture debate citing writers, research and references from both sides of the argument.

Critical writing initially involves a description or summary of published material and provides a range of arguments. However, critical writing then goes further and proceeds to consider the different points of view, going on to make 'a judgment about the information'. Writing critically can also mean using literature to support and evaluate our experiences. For example, a researcher may have observed the different ways that children respond to outdoor learning: 'This proposition is supported by Claxton (2004) who has noted that some children learn better in different contexts, such as the outdoors'.

The overall structure of your research report

The following is a suggestion but depends upon your college/university require-ments and the level of the course you are doing. Most undergraduate projects are approximately 10,000 words whilst a Masters dissertation is more in the region of 15,000–20,000 words. Within your project, each chapter should be able to stand alone as a written piece. Thus each chapter should have an introduction and a conclusion. One of the functions of the introductions and conclusions is to link each chapter to the preceding and following chapter.

Title, author and date

You can have a 'working title' throughout your study and towards the end settle on the final title. Look through article titles in your topic area for suggestions. Your title should be short and to the point. Some titles use a short quote from a research respondent or a phrase which encapsulates the spirit of the study fol-lowed by an explanation of the function of the research, for example, 'School doesn't feel as much of a partnership: Parents' perceptions of their children's transition from nursery school to Reception class' (Shields, 2009) and 'Cinderellas in lonely castles? Perspectives of voluntary preschool supervisors in rural com-munities' (Webster, 2002). These titles work well because the initial part of the title catches the reader's attention whilst the second part, after the colon, explains what the study focuses upon. Notice also how in these titles the methodology is indicated as well as the context for the study.

Acknowledgements

Thank your family and friends for their ideas and support. You should thank the professional colleagues and children in the research institution who gave their time for your study as well as your college supervisor.

Abstract

The abstract is usually the last piece of your project that you write. The function of the abstract is to briefly summarise your research study. The abstract should succinctly state the aim of your research, its methodology and the main find-ings from your research report. The abstract should be no more than 300 words long. Look through the following abstract taken from Polly Shields' (2009) article and identify the issues that she mentions there.

This small-scale study explores a group of English parents' perceptions of their relationships with their child's nursery school and, after the transition to Reception class, their primary school. It references current research and literature on the issues of transition and the role of parents in their children's education. Findings from semi-structured interviews with parents, and with the children's key workers, were analysed for emergent themes. Parents felt very positively about their relationship with their child's nursery, and that they were fully involved in, and informed about, their child's learning. However, the transition to school heralded a change in their relationships. Most parents felt that they had a more distant and less reciprocal relationship with their child's teacher than they had had with their key worker at nursery. The paper concludes with recommendations for further research. (Shields, 2009: 237).

Contents

This should provide a complete rundown of the key headings with page numbers in your study. Each sub-heading can be given a number. For example:

Chapter 1: Introduction

This chapter should include the following:

- the personal and professional reasons for your study
- why the topic is significant
- a brief outline of some of the key arguments
- the research questions
- the overall aims of the study
- an outline of the contents of the remaining chapters in your project.

This introductory chapter is the often the last chapter to be written as then you will know and can present all the different aspects of your project.

Chapter 2: Literature review

The literature review needs to show the relevance of your study and how your study is connected to the ideas and themes within the literature. A literature review is an overall review of the key literature in your topic area. The literature review is concerned with the subject content and academic knowledge of your topic area. Being well read in your chosen topic area is the key to a successful research report. If you are well read and thus knowledgeable in your chosen topic area this will usually transfer into your written work. Being knowledgeable in your area will help your project to focus upon a specific topic, ask the right questions of that area, and provide you with the ability to write an insightful analysis of the data you collect. Hence a thorough literature review is of the utmost importance to a successfully written research study.

The literature review will help you to formulate your research questions by contextualising your research topic in the body of established knowledge. It is important that you are aware of what has already been thought about, researched and written in your interest area. Your research does not sit outside of this established body of knowledge. You need to know how your ideas connect with, build upon and develop what has already been written about in your area. As you read in your area you will make new connections and think about different ways in which you can carry out your research.

A literature review should aim to discuss the definitions of key terms in your chosen topic area. For example, if you were looking at the issue of gender, how is gender defined in the literature? Do sex and gender mean the same thing? If you were looking at the area of inclusion, what does inclusion mean? There are a host of interpretations and understandings of inclusion. Is inclusion the same as special educational needs? You will have to read and reflect upon what different writers say, since such issues in early childhood studies are contested, debated and argued about. Your literature review should reflect the arguments and debates about the issues.

Sources for your literature review

If you are at a college you will have access to an academic library, which is your key resource. Libraries contain various sources of information which will be valuable for your research project. There will be a whole host of available literature in your topic area. Literature is written in a variety of forms for different audiences. In the past week you have probably read a newspaper, a novel, emails and text messages, magazines and perhaps a journal article if you are at college. In a similar way there is a tremendous variety of academic writing and knowledge which is packaged in a variety of ways. Using all the range of literature sources discussed below will ensure a thorough literature review.

Starting off your literature review

The following are three popular ways of starting off your literature review:

1. Looking through back copies of your favourite professional magazine such as *Early Years Educator* or *Nursery World*. Are there any past copies which have a related article in your topic area? If so, does the article have a list of recommended reading or further references to look up and follow through. You should then look on the library's computer system for these books and journal articles, and at the recommended Internet sites. Some of these will be more relevant and interesting than others. Follow up the references from the more interesting ones. These sources may in turn make some useful references which you may wish to follow up. In this way you begin to build up a literature trail leading you to more specialised and focused chapters and articles as you go. Do not be put off if some of the references are not in the library, since you might be able to ask the librarians for inter-library loans to get your book or article.

2. Ask your tutor/supervisor for a reading list in your topic area. What do they suggest you read? Some of your supervisor's recommendations will be more suitable, appealing and relevant than others. Do the useful sources have references which will lead to further sources? Again you are building up a literature trail.

3. Another way to start off your literature review is to carry out an Internet search through a search engine using your key words.

    This may lead you to early years professional websites, journal articles and good practice sites. Some of these can be useful and may lead you to further references and Internet sites. Some professional associations and early years websites are monitored and highly reputable, whilst others are not.

    Be careful not to inadvertently plagiarise material from Internet sites and the online journals. Plagiarism has cost some early years students their degrees, so always make sure you provide thorough references and do not copy or cut and paste any material from the web without indenting it and fully referencing the material.

Additionally, you can search for and read high-quality full-access online articles through the Internet and your college Internet system. Your college librarians can show you how to do this, which usually involves a password taking you through to specific academic search engines.

Potential difficulties

You might find that the area you have chosen for your research appears to have a limited number of references. If this is the case, it might be that your research questions are too specific and need broadening out. In any case, at the beginning of a literature search it is good practice to read widely in the field. You will generate new ideas that you might later be able to integrate into your study. For example, if you were interested in the area of mixed heritage young children and how their identities are supported in a nursery you might find little literature. It is often difficult to find a large number of references which are very similar to your title (Oliver, 2004). You would need to broaden out the key words from mixed heritage to include race and ethnicity generally, and include all children not just the early years. You would need to look at the legislation around the issue of race too. Your computer searching might lead you to just one or two specific articles or books on mixed heritage children that you can only access through inter-library loans. You would need to wait for this material and broaden out your search as suggested above to widen the whole issue more generally. With the case above, perhaps examining how young children's identities are supported generally in a nursery might be a more doable piece of research and the issue of mixed race would be but one of a number of issues that arise, along with family, the community, class, gender, geographical location, religion and ethnicity and how nurseries accommodate such differences.

The opposite of this problem is that you may have found you have too much material. For example, your research area might be literacy in the early years, in which case you would be overwhelmed by the volumes of literature on the subject. In this case you need to narrow down your research interests and questions. For example, you might narrow your focus to include only boys and literacy in the early years or only girls and literacy in the early years. An alternative way of focusing might be on specific forms of literacy such as media literacy and the early years. Such a process of carefully examining the key words in your research area and refining them will lead to a focused literature review and study.

Activity

This activity is based upon the following extract taken from Min Siew Yap's (2010) small-scale survey which aimed to find out more about Malaysian parents' perspectives of pre-school education in Kuala Lumpur.

As you read the following edited extract from Min Siew's literature review, answer the following questions:

What has she done to set the scene?
How has she structured her arguments?
What issues has she raised in these opening paragraphs?
How has she related the literature review to her own study?

Literature Review Introduction

This chapter will begin with an introduction of Malaysian society and will analyse the policy development of pre-school education in Malaysia, in particular, the National Pre-school Curriculum. Parents' perspectives of pre-school education will be discussed through a critical analysis of previous international studies of parents' beliefs, perceptions and expectations of children's learning and early years education (Bryson et al. 2006; Hewitt & Maloney 2000; Marjory 1995). These studies are discussed in relation to the Malaysian context.

Parental views on pre-school education

With regard to Malaysian parents' perceptions of pre-school education, a study by Hewitt & Maloney (2000) examined the potential influence of socio-cultural elements on parents' perceptions of pre-school education in Malaysia. On one hand, parents' ideal reason for sending children to pre-school was the role it played in children's social-emotional development and in preparation for formal schooling. Similarly, the results for parents' views on 'pre-school education goals' showed social domain goals to be more popular than intellectual domain goals (Hewitt & Maloney 2000). On the other hand, when related to the broader socio-cultural context and children's needs in the future, parents tended to emphasise the academic domain. Most of the parents saw preparation for Standard one first year in Malaysian primary education, academically, socially and emotionally, as the main actual purpose of pre-school education. Furthermore, learning to read and teacher-directed instruction in phonics and the alphabet, counting and mathematics were considered as very important learning experiences in pre-school by the majority of parents (Hewitt &

Maloney 2000). According to Hewitt & Maloney (2000), many parents appeared to be torn between their idealised (social orientated) and actualised (academic orientated) perceptions. Finally, it was predicted that increased contact and communication between parents, pre-school teachers and policy makers could assist in narrowing the gap between parents' idealised and actualised perceptions (Hewitt & Maloney 2000).

Bryson et al. (2006) interviewed 8000 parents in England to provide information on parents' use, views and experiences of childcare and early years provision. It was found that most parents used formal childcare and early years provision for educational reasons in relation to the child's educational development, whilst others were for economic reasons that related to parents' work and studies (Bryson et al. 2006). Overall, parents in this study were largely positive about the quality of the early years provision in England. However, a significant number of parents felt that there was a lack of information about the early years provision, the cost and the quality of provision (Bryson et al. 2006).

Foot et al. (2000) researched Scottish parents' preferences, beliefs, knowledge and expectations when choosing suitable early years provision. The parents regarded that the most important issues were the happiness of a child and safety and security, followed by the quality of care and the attitudes of staff. The parents' expectations were said to be based on their own educational experiences (Foot et al. 2000). It was concluded that although 'happiness' and 'safety and security' feature highly in most parents' reasons for choice, some parents assumed that these are 'given' and instead focused on other reasons for their choice of setting. The research highlighted the issue of partnership between parents and service providers as crucial for providing high quality provision (Foot et al. 2000).

In Hong Kong, Marjory (1995) conducted a study with 100 Chinese parents and 100 Chinese teachers to elicit their views on the purposes of early childhood education. It was reported that teachers and parents ranked socialisation as the most important purpose, followed by 'preparation for formal schooling' as Hong Kong parents would expect their children to acquire knowledge and skills in kindergartens. Marjory (1995) highlighted some significant differences in the expressed views of both parents and teachers, for example, some teachers disagreed with parents who would expect 'homework' for pre-school children whilst undervaluing the role of activities in developing children's thinking and physical skills. Hence, it was noted that parents and teachers should work together to understand the views of one another as good parent–teacher relationships usually result in more effective pre-schooling for children (Marjory 1995, page 17).

(Continued)

(Continued)

References

Bryson, C., Kazimirski, A., Southwood, H. (2006) *Childcare and early years provision: a study of parents' use, views and experience.* Nottingham: DfES Publications.

Foot, H., Howe, C., Bheyne, B., Terras, M., Rattray, C. (2000) Pre-school education: parents' preferences, knowledge and expectations. *International Journal of Early Years Education*, 8(3), 189–204.

Hewitt, B., Maloney, C. (2000) Malaysian parents' ideal and actual perceptions of pre-school education. *International Journal of Early Years Education*, 8(1), 83–92.

Marjory, E. (1995) Purposes of early childhood education: expressed views of teachers and parents in Hong Kong. *International Journal of Early Years Education*, 3(2), 3–18.

Chapter 3: Methodology

In this chapter you should re-state your research questions and the central aim of your study. This is because you will need to demonstrate how your research questions have determined the research design and methods and the analysis. In this chapter you should *justify* why you have chosen the particular research design for your project. This chapter should also report upon the ethical practices that you employed in your study.

Chapter 4: Findings

This chapter is where you can present your findings in a variety of tables and charts and diagrams. Each table will need labelling. It is possible to collapse the findings and the discussion chapters into one chapter. If you have considerable amounts of data that you wish to present and draw the main themes from then it is best to have separate chapters.

Chapter 5: Discussion

The discussion should provide an analysis of the findings. The discussion might, for example, be structured according to the themes which emerged from your data. The analysis and discussion of the data should use the relevant literature already presented in your literature review and may also include new literature.

Chapter 6: Conclusions

The following questions will help to structure your conclusion:

- What tentative and cautious conclusions can you make from your small-scale research project?

- How does your study build upon/question/develop existing knowledge in this area?

- What reflections can you make about what worked well and what did not work well during the research process?

- What reflections can you make about your relationships with your research participants?

- What different and further questions would you ask if you were doing this project again?

- What could you do to improve your study?

Many researchers at the end of their projects are acutely aware of what they could have done better. This is because much research generates further questions for future investigation. Early childhood is such a complex area that research in the discipline frequently raises more questions than answers. It is important that you acknowledge that you have not provided *all* the answers in your early childhood research area and that your research is small scale and cannot provide generalisations beyond the context of the research itself.

References

Writing out references is tedious and time-consuming but it is part of the academic requirements and it must be correctly carried out. This is because within academia knowledge is slowly accumulated and passed on from generation to generation. Respect must be given to those whose research and hard work you have used to build your own ideas and work. Original ideas are rare, hence the necessity for full references. It is equally important that you follow very carefully your own institution's rules as regards the details of how to present references. Each institution is different and you will be penalised if you do not follow the prescribed style correctly. Many colleges and universities use the Harvard Referencing style. Sheffield University Library provides an up-to-date overview of the Harvard Referencing style (http://www.shef.ac.uk/library/libdocs/hsl-dvc1.pdf).

Appendices

Within the appendices you can place copies of children's pictures, questionnaire examples, interview transcriptions and information about the early childhood institution. Please remember that the appendices are for non-essential information and that your tutor does not have to read these.

Avoiding plagiarism

It is very important that you do not copy other people's work without referencing it properly, as Yap has done in the extract quoted above. If you feel under pressure of time it might seem tempting to try to pass off somebody else's work as your own. This is known as plagiarism and is treated as a serious offence. Within the academic world it is equivalent to stealing others' work. Depending upon the severity of the plagiarism, it is possible that you may be asked to leave the course and lose your qualification and degree. With the use of the Internet it is increasingly tempting to try to pass off others' work as your own. However, your tutors can usually quickly spot this work as not being your own writing. Additionally, much student work is now uploaded onto a network. Your research project is then checked through for plagiarism electronically and if you have plagiarised, it will be discovered. Hence it is not worth it. Better to write your own material and carefully and thoroughly reference it.

The responsibilities of your supervisor

If you are doing your research project at a college then you will probably be assigned a supervisor for the duration of your research. The supervisor may have chosen you as one of their students because they have expertise, current knowledge and interest concerning your particular topic area. Equally, you may have chosen a particular supervisor because of such issues. The professional and academic relationship between supervisor and student demands that both have certain duties, roles and responsibilities that they should perform. At the heart of the relationship is a desire from both the supervisor and the student to get the research project successfully completed on time.

The supervisor has a number of responsibilities including:

• giving advice about the suitability and appropriateness of your research topic
• commenting on the ethical dilemmas

- discussing suitable methods

- suggesting literature sources

- setting up a timetable of tutorials

- reading the student's work and giving appropriate feedback

- listening to, asking questions of and advising the student on the progress of their research study

- ensuring that the student produces sufficient high-quality work to meet the college's academic requirements. This will include providing the student with detailed guidance on the overall structure of the research report.

Your responsibilities throughout the research

Just as your supervisor has a number of responsibilities so, too, do you. These can include the following:

- prioritising college responsibilities including attendance at pre-arranged tutorials

- identifying your interest area

- reading and writing throughout the project at the appropriate level

- honestly sharing anxiety and excitement concerning the project

- emailing work in well ahead of tutorials so the supervisor has sufficient time to make comments

- locating and making access arrangements to an early childhood setting in which to carry out your study

- listening to and acting upon your supervisor's advice

- sticking to the agreed timetable to ensure submission by the deadline.

The research tutorial

Honest and open discussion, without ambiguity, is necessary for a successful relationship between supervisor and student. Helpful discussions can be organised by using a college tutorial pro forma such as in Figure 5.1.

One of the key issues on the pro forma includes what the student has done since the last meeting under the heading of 'Progress since last tutorial'.

Early Childhood Studies

Supervision of Independent Study Tutorial Form

Name of Student

Name of Tutor

Date and Time

Topic of Independent Study

Progress since last tutorial

1.

2.

3.

4.

5.

Agreed Action – to be completed by next meeting

1.

2.

3.

4.

5.

Agreed Date of Next Meeting

Student Sign/Date

Tutor Sign/Date

Figure 5.1   A college tutorial pro forma

Depending upon the stage of the research project, this might include all or some of the following: reading and writing for the literature review; carrying out fieldwork in the research setting; analysing the data. Reading and writing throughout the duration of the project is certainly a good habit to get into. It will help you successfully to complete the project on time. Pass written drafts to your tutor in good time ahead of the tutorial. This gives your supervisor sufficient time to make comments on your written work ahead of the tutorial. It is your responsibility to ensure that any 'agreed action' is done by the next tutorial.

The pro forma is copied and emailed so that both supervisor and student have agreed and signed notes of the tutorial. The actual number of tutorial meetings is normally fixed by your college. Perhaps six such meetings *for such a research project* are sufficient.

Your research timetabling

Your supervisor must advise not only on the content of your work, but also on its timetabling to ensure successful completion *on time*. Hence the importance of your preparation for and attendance at tutorials as well as carrying out the 'agreed action'. This is all done to help you to achieve your goal – meeting the research project's submission date. When starting off your project, the deadline, perhaps next spring, seems an eternity away. However, time has a habit of speeding up the closer the deadline approaches, hence the importance of planning an agreed timetable with your supervisor.

A typical year's research project is shown in Table 5.1.

Table 5.1   A typical research project timetable

To do	Month
Thinking about topic, reading and planning	Spring and summer months
Submit research plan	October
Access research setting	November
Write ongoing literature review	November/December
Carry out fieldwork	December
Analyse data	February/March
Write up study	February/March
Submit your research study	End of March

Summary ▢

In this chapter you have:

- examined how to write a convincing critical argument
- gained an overview of the organisation and structure of your project

(Continued)

(Continued)

- reflected upon how to successfully use the library's resources for your literature review

- raised your awareness of how to structure and write a literature review

- appreciated the dangers of plagiarism

- seen how to correctly reference your literature sources.

Recommended reading 📖

Blaxter, L., Christina, H. and Tight, M. (2006) *How to Research*. Buckingham: Open University Press.
Chapter 4 has excellent suggestions on doing your literature review.

Punch, K. (2009) *Introduction to Research Methods in Education*. London: Sage Publications.
Chapter 15 of this thorough and detailed research methods textbook provides an easy-to-use guide to the whole process of research writing. It also includes advice on structuring and organising your research outline.

http://caplitswritingcentre.ioe.ac.uk/dissertations.html
This website, based at the Institute of Education, University of London, demonstrates the key structural features of a dissertation.

6

Observation: looking and listening

Learning objectives

This chapter will help you to:

- understand that observations include looking and *listening*
- have an understanding of why researchers use observations
- be aware of the problem of interpretation when carrying out observations
- know *how* to watch and listen with an open and critical mind
- begin to understand the difficulties of observation
- identify the different kinds of observations
- ways to record your observations
- study examples of different kinds of observations.

Why do observations?

Observations are one of the most frequently used forms of first-hand evidence collection that early childhood researchers make. Early childhood professionals are now experienced in the use of observations as part of their professional working lives. The Early Years Foundation Stage (DCSF, 2008) expects professionals to carry out systematic observations of the young children in their care. This chapter builds upon that experience by framing observations within the context of a research project. Early childhood researchers are continuously making observations during visits to the institutions in which they are carrying out their research. Researchers are always looking and listening for information and behaviour which will help them to answer their research questions.

It is important to note that observations are frequently combined with other research methods. Thus, when carrying out interviews, drawings or questionnaires, the researcher is also making observations of the children, practitioners and parents in the setting. This chapter explores the ways in which those observations can be systematically made.

 Activity

The following are some quotes from students who carried out observations for their research projects. They give a variety of reasons for doing observations.

Which of the reasons below do you think might be appropriate for you? Why?

'You actually get out to see and listen to the children, the practitioners, the parents in a real life situation.'
'It's very interesting because you can see what people actually do, rather than what they say they do!'
'What they say they do and what they actually do is not always the same.'
'The observations gave me a "feel" for the nursery. I was welcomed in and told that my research was needed. It felt so good.'
'Just sitting there watching and listening to all the activities for a day gave me such a good idea of the rhythm and pattern of daily life in the Reception class.'
'Observations gave me lots of ideas about what to actually ask the children later on in the interviews.'
'I got a very good understanding of the place by shadowing my mate for a week.'

'The more time I spent in the nursery, the more I understood why they do things in a certain way.'

'It was difficult because, although I tried to be "a fly on the wall", the children kept asking me questions.'

'I learnt so much just by watching and listening.'

What is observation?

At the heart of observation is 'seeing' familiar and routine events in the early childhood setting in a new way (Clough and Nutbrown, 2007). For example, have you ever had the experience of being on holiday and then coming back home and seeing everyday things that you always took for granted in a different way? In Britain it is taken for granted that we drive on the left-hand side of the road, but if you have been abroad you might question this so-called normal practice. Driving on the left might feel strange for a few days. Can you think of other cultural practices that feel strange when you return home?

In a similar way critical looking and listening in research demands that you try to make familiar everyday behaviour that seems 'normal', distant and strange. By making everyday events unfamiliar and foreign to you, you will be engaging in critical observation. Through your readings and your observations you should try to open up and see everyday situations that you take as being normal in a different light.

Interpretation

Have you ever had the experience of being at a party and then talking about it the following day with your friend? Have you noticed how you will have experienced and interpreted the same event in different ways? You were both there and probably both talked to the same people but may have come away with different perspectives and understandings of what happened. You have to talk together to make sense of your shared experience which you have interpreted in different ways. Whether you can see the whole picture or only part of the picture demonstrates a dilemma for researchers; different researchers see different things. Researchers are rarely able to see the whole picture in all its complexity and only ever get a partial view. This is because early childhood researchers interpret social situations and events in different ways depending upon their assumptions, beliefs and values derived from our previous experiences. Our age, gender, sexuality, ethnicity and class all help to form our experiences of life. These varied experiences influence our perceptions and interpretation of events (Rolfe and Emmett, 2010).

So 'seeing and telling it like it is' becomes highly problematic. Thus, checking out other people's perspectives and interpretations of situations is critical for a researcher. This is why triangulation, that is the collection of different perspectives, is critical in adding to the validity of the research. With triangulated methods, the perceptions and interpretations of others, such as the children, the practitioners and the parents, are listened to. Acknowledging your assumptions and biases through a reflexive approach will further help to validate your observations (Rolfe and Emmett, 2010).

Being open in your looking and listening

The *way* in which you watch and listen is important. Looking and listening in research involves more than everyday looking and listening. Looking and listening in research involves:

- looking radically
- looking critically
- looking openly
- looking for evidence
- looking for information
- looking for things we sometimes understand and sometimes do not understand
- looking to be persuaded.

    (adapted from Clough and Nutbrown, 2007)

Looking radically and critically and in an open manner means you are prepared to suspend your assumptions and biases and try to see things from a different perspective. If you are looking critically and openly then you will be more ready to see your research topic in a new and different light. This might happen as you watch and listen to the events in the institution in which you are carrying out your research. Looking critically does not mean that you are criticising for the sake of it, but rather in the light of your reading on the topic asking yourself why people are behaving in the ways that they do. Looking in these different ways involves watching and listening to all the events around you in an *active* way. It is about being open as to *why* children, practitioners and parents are doing things in a different way from that which you might expect.

Being aware of, listening to, recording and reflecting upon the different points of view you observe and hear is the critical essence of research observations. Indeed, observing and listening to alternative possibilities about your topic of interest might *transform* your current understanding of the topic. This involves listening, in the widest sense, to different 'voices' about the topic. Sometimes we hold strong views on issues which research or systematic inquiry might change. Thus, opening up and listening to and watching alternative ways may lead us to question those strong beliefs and assumptions. Trying to see the world from somebody else's perspective is an important aspect of research. Only when the researcher begins systematically to take into account these alternative ways of seeing the topic does mere inquisitiveness change into research (Clough and Nutbrown, 2007).

Knowing the context of your research setting

One of the important ways in which researchers can open up and begin to see and hear different perspectives of their topic is to have a good understanding of the context of the institution in which they are working. Different institutions operate in different ways, depending upon their location and contexts.

 Activity

The following questions will help you to build up your knowledge about the wider context of the early childhood institution in which you are making your observations.

What is the socio-economic context of the neighbourhood?
Is it a well-to-do or poor or mixed neighbourhood?

(Continued)

(Continued)

Are the parents/carers professional, skilled or unskilled workers?
What is the history of the early childhood institution?
What are the sources of funding for the institution?
How many children are on roll? What ages are they?
How many days are the children at the centre?
What ethnicities are present in the institution?
What languages do the children/families speak?
What is the gender balance?
How many staff are there?
What is the turnover amongst the staff?

In the following example, I was interested in the issue of inclusion in a nursery. The wider context of the nursery was noted, as were the immediate entrance and my first feelings at being in the building:

> The nursery is surrounded by expensive new apartment blocks with balconies, landscaped gardens and in-house leisure facilities. These have been built in the last ten years to house the nearby burgeoning financial sector workers. These apartment blocks are in 'gated communities' which have high walls and large gates serving to exclude the long standing local community and their children who attend the local school and its attached nursery. Although the school is surrounded by such ostentatious economic wealth, 73% of the pupils are entitled to free school meals, which is well above the national average and is an indication of the high unemployment and poverty experienced by the school community (Bradshaw, 2001). The local families rent flats in the nearby council tower blocks. It would seem that the local community does not benefit from the surrounding economic wealth. The headteacher confirmed this observation and stated that 'the children's poverty actually has the effect of excluding them from the local cafés, shops and restaurants. The builders even want the local park for new expensive flats.'

> Once in the nursery however, the high, cold and hard exclusionary walls that surround the school and its locale are transformed. Next to the welcome poster, translated into the children's twelve languages is a wall covered in the photographs and names of the children and the staff in the school. The staff are representative of the different linguistic communities of the families. From floor to

ceiling are large pictures that the children have recently painted. Such an entrance presents a welcome, safe and inclusive environment in stark contrast to the exclusionary feel outside the nursery's front door. A 'Family Room' is located off this entrance hall with armchairs, children's books, including dual language texts and toys (Clarke and Siraj-Blatchford, 2000). Drinks facilities are also located in here. Once again the many languages of the school are represented on the walls of the Family Room. This serves to include the local families. As I met the nursery headteacher she presented me with a coffee and stated that the research about inclusion was timely and needed to be done. I felt at ease and was told that I would be introduced to all the staff and the children. (Roberts-Holmes, 2001:7)

The above broad-brush descriptive piece gives an overview of the nursery school, its immediate surroundings and how I felt about my first impressions on being in the nursery. The unstructured and anecdotal observations are given validity by the headteacher's comments and the references to supportive literature.

Unstructured observations

In an early years setting there are literally hundreds of interactions going on all the time around you: practitioners talking with each other and the children, the children talking and learning with each other, parents coming and going, children moving around different activities, some children getting attention whilst others are being ignored. For the first-time researcher it is all rather daunting. What are you going to focus upon?

To begin with you can be fairly non-selective in your observations. This unfocused looking and listening is known as unstructured observations. In your unfocused observations you should try to get an overall feel for the situation. Go with 'the flow' of the institution and make broad-brush notes about your feelings in your notebook. It might not always be possible to note down everything that you see, hear and feel about your research setting because your notebook might not always be to hand. Hence the importance of reflecting upon all that you have seen and heard in your research setting as soon as you get home. Important feelings and thoughts are quickly lost if a note is not made of them the same day. These notes are known as anecdotal records and provide valuable background information on the research setting. These anecdotal observations and records provide evidence of your ongoing reflective research diary.

Structured observations

As you become familiar with the institution, you should progressively focus upon specific structured observations. Keeping your overall research questions in mind will help you to do so.

- What do you want to research and why?

- What is the purpose of the observation?

- What is the focus of the observation?

- How will you stay focused?

When carrying out structured observations it is critical to be *focused* and to know exactly what you wish to look for. A good knowledge of the literature in your area will help you to know what to focus upon. From reading in your area you will know what is significant and important and what is not significant and not important for your study. It is imperative that you keep your overall research questions in mind when carrying out observations (Clough and Nutbrown, 2007). If you have little time for your study, you should be asking yourself, how is what I am watching going to add to my research study? Early childhood researchers use the following to help structure their observations, including tally counting, target child observation schedules, event sampling and target child running records, video observation and maps and diagrams.

Tally counting

As a part of Katy's structured observations for her project on how nurseries support ethnic diversity, she made a systematic inventory of each nursery's resources. Specifically, she made a tally of the range of resources, including puzzles, books, dressing-up clothes, play food and posters on the wall, that reflected ethnic and linguistic diversity in each of the two nurseries. This meant, for example, that she had to analyse all the books in each nursery in terms of their ethnic representation.

Figure 6.1 shows the number of books that represented diverse ethnic cultures in their pictures and storylines.

The tally chart below indicates how many of the books in the nursery setting show characters from different cultures and races . . .	
Characters in book are:	**Number of books:**
Mono-cultural (white)	JHT JHT JHT JHT JHT JHT JHT JHT III
Mono-cultural (black)	IIII
Mono-cultural (Asian)	I
Multi-cultural	JHT JHT JHT JHT JHT JHT JHT JHT JHT JHT
Dual-language	JHT I — 3 – farsi & English 3 – Somali & English.

Figure 6.1   **The number of books that represented diverse ethnic cultures in their pictures and storylines**

Observation schedules

Observation schedules help the researcher to focus upon a child or group of children or practitioner, and to attempt systematically to answer a series of specific questions. See Figures 6.2, 6.3 and 6.4

What is the child doing? What is the child saying? Where is the child looking? Who is the child looking at? Who does the child speak to? What does the child say? What questions does the child ask? Who answers the questions?

Figure 6.2   **Listening and looking: a target child observation schedule (Lancaster and Broadbent, 2010)**

Who is doing what?

Who is saying what?

What do the children play with?

Who do the children play with?

Who do the children speak to?

What do the children say?

Who asks the questions?

Who answers them?

Figure 6.3   An observational schedule of a group of children playing (Lancaster and Broadbent, 2010)

Who is the observer?

Where does observation take place?

Who is being observed?

Age of child/ren:

Purpose of observation:

Date:

Time	Who is present	What is happening?	Who is the child looking at?	What is being said/Who is saying it?

Figure 6.4   An observation record sheet (adapted from Lancaster and Broadbent, 2010: 15)

Activity

Consider the following case study:

What were Gary's overall research questions?
What structured observation techniques does Gary use?

Case study

How do three-year-olds socialise?

Gary's research questions were based upon how 2- and 3-year-old children socially interact together. He wanted to know how some of these children who were pre-verbal made sense of their playing together. The practitioner told him to focus upon a 3-year-old called Pam. Gary made a number of observations of Pam in different contexts, the example in Figure 6.5 being made in the garden. Gary had visited the playgroup three times and was known to the parents, children and staff, and it had been agreed that he carry out these observations as part of his college study.

Gary found that the children were so interested in playing with him that it was difficult for him to write down his observations. He found that if he played with the children for 20 minutes or so and then observed them for concentrated short bursts of 10 minutes then he was more likely to be successful. The children soon realised that he was not playing any more and left him alone.

In the observation (Figure 6.5) it can be seen that, even though the 3-year-olds hardly spoke, they were fully participating together in the activities. Gary noticed in his observation that Pam spent time looking at what other children were doing and then copied them. He noticed this in her drawing and modelling activities too. Gary's observations confirmed that much of young children's play is highly sociable (Moyles, 1993).

Observation Record Sheet:
Who is the observer? Gary
Where does observation take place? Hill View Children's Centre, garden area.
Who is being observed? Pam
Age of child/ren: Three
Purpose of observation: Nature of social interactions that Pam engages in.
Date: 10.5.04

Time	Who is present	What is happening?	Who is the child looking at?	What is being said/Who is saying it?
10.10	P and J	J is using a toy lawnmower.	P watching her.	
10.11	P and J		J.	
10.12	P and J	P gets another toy lawnmower	J.	
10.14		Follows J round the garden.	Me	P 'look at all the colours'.
		P bumps lawnmower into me		
10.15	P and J and S			
10.16	S, P and J	P leaves lawnmower and picks up car to play with.		
10.17	S, P and J	S takes the lawnmower	J racing P with the lawnmower.	
		P plays with toy car. S chasing J with the lawnmower		
10.19	S, P and J, Practitioner		Practitioner gives the lawnmower to P.	P shouting at S 'it's mine, it's mine'.
		P climbs on rocking horse with wheels and races up and down wooden decking	Races Jane with her lawnmower.	J and P laughing together as they run.
10.20	S, P and J, Practitioner			
		Pam gets off rocking horse and retrieves her lawnmower by pulling it from S.		
		P goes with lawnmower to the wooden decking		

Figure 6.5   Gray's record observation sheet for Pam

Event sampling and running records

Sarah's research questions were concerned with the ways in which a child's gender influenced their friendships. Sarah's observations were focused because she concentrated upon looking and listening to gender-influenced behaviour that she had read about. Such a focus upon particular or targeted behaviour is known as event sampling. When the targeted behaviour occurred Sarah noted it down long-hand.

Sarah carried out a running record of the gendered interactions. A running record is a descriptive account of everything that Sarah saw and heard concerning that behaviour. In the course of one day she noted down 25 friendship observations which centred upon gendered behaviour. Sarah used a coding system for her observations to save time rather than writing down the full names:

Running record one

T = teacher

I = Isabelle

L = Lucy

T: Approaches the table and asks the girls what colour card they would like to make their litter posters on. I chooses pink so does L. I and L pick up a pencil and begin to draw.

L: 'What are you doing?'

I: 'I am drawing a picture of a rubbish bin. See like this!' I shows L her drawing.

L: 'Oh yeah!' The girls are sitting closer together. I and L get on with their respective drawings in silence for about a minute.

I: 'Can you do an "r" for me?'. I leans over and writes an 'r' on L's poster.

'Oh, I didn't know how to do that because I thought you did it another way'.

I laughs and L joins in laughing too.

Running record two

A = Anna

P = Peter

At playtime Anna is the only girl who consistently wants to play football with the boys. Anna and Peter were sitting next to each other reading on the carpet looking at a Preston Pig book concerning football.

A: 'I like football and I'm really good at it.'

P: 'Yer it's true you are good but I'm the best.'

A: 'So what team do you support then?'

P: 'West Ham 'cos they're the best. What do you support?'

A: 'Gillingham and I'm gonna play for them too'.

Both the above running records of the targeted behaviour demonstrate inter-esting qualities about how gendered behaviour reinforced and confirmed friendship. In the first observation, the two girls displayed compliant and positive helpful friendship (Thorne, 1993). In her research report Sarah reflected upon how her observations had changed some of the children's behaviour.

Video observations

Some researchers have found making videos of children a useful observational technique. There are particular ethical difficulties when using cameras and video (see Chapters 3 and 8). Permission must be gained from all the research participants, who should also be told exactly what use is to be made of the video, who will see it, where the video will be kept and for how long (Willan, 2004). As you read the following example taken from Gill's research experiences with young children, can you list the advantages and disadvantages associated with using video recorders?

> I tried taking notes about the naturally occuring children's maths activities but found that was impossible. Very young children are not static enough because they just keep moving around and changing activities a lot. I found I couldn't keep up with them and write fast enough. I wasn't getting everything down that I wanted to. I also felt the note taking was quite intrusive because the children were interested in what I was writing. So I had a go at videoing and I found that the children didn't take much notice of the camera at all. You can hold it on your lap too, so it's not too intrusive. I handheld it the whole time. They get used to it and treat it like an appendage – they just ignored it after a while. What's really great about video is that you get all the context too, which is very difficult to do with writing. You can't capture the whole context with note taking but with video you can. I needed that context because the maths was so embedded into the play, that only by rewatching the video was I able to see the maths.

Whilst Gill found that the children were not particularly interested in the video-taping and that it did not interfere too much with their activities, Rolfe and Emmett (2010: 323) found that using videos was 'highly intrusive'. This may be due to the closeness of the relationship between researcher and child rather than the video camera itself. The major advantage of video-taping is that particular sequences can be replayed again and again so that fine behavioural details and subtleties can be noted and interpreted (Rolfe and Emmett, 2010). Transcribing video footage does take considerable skill and time but is rewarding since the whole context is captured on tape and can be discussed in the transcription.

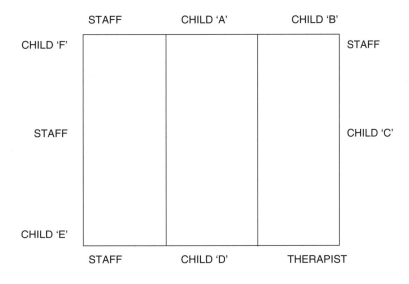

Figure 6.6   An observational diagram

Observational diagrams

Elaine's study was concerned with the use of group therapy sessions in speech and language sessions. One of the observational techniques she used included the use of mapping the participants during a therapy session, as shown in Figure 6.6.

Figure 6.6 is a powerful observational technique because it clearly shows how the children C, D, E and F are separated from each other by the practitioners (staff) and the therapist. It is an irony that the adults themselves are acting as a barrier to the children's collaborative participation in the group therapy session.

Interestingly, in Elaine's study it was the practitioners and not the children who were affected by her presence. One of the practitioners kept leaning over to Elaine and half jokingly made comments such as 'I hope you didn't write that down!' and 'Don't tell them we do that when you get back to college'. Elaine assured the practitioner of the confidentiality of her study through anonymising the name of the institution. Elaine also left a report of the study with the institution. It is important to note that professionals often feel that they are being assessed and judged, and the researcher should be sensitive to the ways in which the observations may change the professionals' behaviour. Elaine attempted to alleviate this particular practitioner's anxiety by showing her all the observation notes at the end of each session.

Participant observation

In this sort of observation the researcher actually participates and joins in with the children and the practitioners in their daily routine and activities. They become involved and included in the actual situation or event that they are researching. Through experiencing the activity for themselves the researcher is able to *understand* the research topic at first hand. The researcher is an insider because he or she fully participates in the event that is being studied (Denscombe, 2007). The depth of involvement varies between researchers and research projects, but common to all participant observers is the large amount of time needed.

The key to good participant observation is to spend a lot of time with the children and practitioners. The better the researcher knows the context, the practitioners, the children and parents, the richer the quality of data and evidence that will be collected. Where the researcher is well known, she or he is more likely to be able to understand the detail, the subtleties and the complexities of the situation. Developing these relationships takes *considerable* time and, so, the researcher should be prepared to spend large amounts of time inside and outside the research setting developing these all-important relationships. Usually the more time spent in the research setting the better the quality of evidence.

Activity

Observation checklist

The following questions are designed to encourage *reflection* about your use of observations.

In what ways did observations help you to answer your research questions?
Did you use structured and unstructured observations? Why?
How did you know what to observe?
How did your presence affect the children?
How did the observations affect you?
What were the ethical considerations of your observations?
What were the problems and difficulties in doing the observations?

The following case study research arose from a concern that my 4-year-old son, Jake, might be watching too many children's videos and thus I feared that his creativity and imagination might be suffering, as suggested by Barker and Petley (2001). This concern was transformed when I observed Jake's play after he had watched his videos. I was a participant observer in the research because I was fully engaged with my son's play, rather than a distant and removed observer.

Case study

I attempted to understand what *meaning* the video stories had for Jake in his play (Pahl, 1999). As I played with Jake I made detailed notes on the characters, toys and storylines. I reflected upon how the play was influenced by the videos. I scribbled Jake's play narrative down on paper at the time Jake was playing and later transcribed and analysed it. I continued this participant observation for over three months at home and in his nursery.

The evidence that I collected from such participatory observations suggested that Jake would play with his wooden train set and 're-make' the video storylines and narratives in new and imaginative ways. The video storylines would be reworked with new engines, new situations and other characters from different popular videos. An imaginative interweaving of plots and children's characters would emerge in this play. Thus, for example, Thomas was helped by Spiderman to ensure that Postman Pat's letters were all delivered on time! Other family members and his key worker at nursery reported that Jake's playing sometimes contained narratives from popular television shows. These different 'voices' in different contexts added validity to the findings. The mini research project pointed towards videos potentially being a *stimulus* and an important facilitator for children's creative and imaginative play (Buckingham, 1993). My initial biases and apprehensions were contradicted by the research.

As a participant observer I was able to join in with Jake's play and gain detailed *insider* evidence and insight into his play. By recording the narrative that went with the play I was able to note the detail, complexity and interconnectedness with the videos. At times Jake did not like my making notes because he said 'writing stuff down is not proper playing'. Hence I had to write the notes up later. By knowing Jake and his context so well I was able to place his play within a rich context.

Summary

This chapter has:

- discussed why researchers do observations
- shown you unstructured and structured ways to carry out observations
- discussed *how* to look and listen critically
- provided examples of various observational techniques.

Recommended reading 📖

Palaiologou, I. (2008) *Childhood Observation (Achieving EYPS)*. Exeter: Learning Matters.

This book has been specifically written for professionals who are expected to carry out systematic observations of children within the Early Years Foundation Stage. It has very clear coverage of the different observational methods and is invaluable for the beginner early childhood researcher.

Rolfe, S. and Emmett, S. (2010) 'Direct observation', in MacNaughton, G., Rolfe, S. and Siraj-Blatchford, I. (eds), *Doing Early Childhood Research: International Perspectives on Theory and Practice*, 2nd edn. Buckingham: Open University Press.

The chapter provides a very clear overview of the role of observations with early childhood education and embeds the discussion within a detailed case study which used observations.

7

Creative listening to young children

Learning objectives

This chapter will help you to:

- have a greater awareness of the many ways in which young children are able to express themselves
- be familiar with the connections between research and increased children's participation
- understand different ways of listening to young children
- understand how children can act as co-researchers
- understand the methods of the Mosaic approach.

Developing cultures of meaningful participation

It is excellent to see that listening to young children is now at the heart of The Early Years Foundation Stage (DCSF, 2008). Genuine listening is core to the four themes of the Early Years Foundation Stage. As such this represents a significant advance for children and their participation with early years settings. Your research can work with the ideology of listening to children that is central to the Early Years Foundation Stage.

The agenda for increasing children's participation in their services has come from three main directions. First, there is the notion that children are consumers of services, and, just like other consumers, children's voices need to be heard too. Second, children used to be identified as part of a family or care facility and were rarely identified as a group in their own right. Children's needs and wants were interpreted by the adults around them, who spoke for children. The third main influence on children's participation has come from the UN Convention on the Rights of the Child (UN, 1989) discussed in the ethics chapter. The participation agenda demands a cultural shift away from working *for* children to working *with* children.

Meaningful participation requires a cultural shift by the childcare organisation away from a one-off listening event to a *sustainable* participatory culture. Such a shift occurs when children's views and opinions are embedded within the principles of mutual trust and respect between children and adults. The children (and adults) need to see that their ideas are not only listened to but also *acted* upon. Listening to children is only half the story. Acting upon children's input is the other half of the story. Unless action is seen to be taken, the children will perhaps correctly assume that such participation is tokenistic practice (Kirby et al., 2003).

If at an early age children are encouraged to participate in decisions that affect their daily lives in their environments and see that such an input has real effects, then these same children are more likely to engage in participation as they get older. Engaging with the children in a participatory research project may be part of a wider institutional cultural change in which inclusion and participation become embedded in the daily thinking and practice of children's environments.

The following is a list of reasons as to why young children should be involved in participatory research projects (adapted from Kirby et al., 2003: 19):

Practical benefits to early childhood settings

- Improved levels of care and education

- Improved support to ensure individuals' best interests (e.g. enhanced learning, improved health, increased opportunities for play)

- Improved experience of services (e.g. increased emotional well-being, reduced stress and feelings of insecurity)

- Improved access to and use of services

- Improved service accountability.

Citizenship and social inclusion

- Providing inclusive practice that draws in those often excluded (e.g. young children, carers, asylum seekers and disabled young children)

- Meeting expectations for children's right to participate in decisions affecting their lives

- Empowering children through being included

- Developing skills and knowledge to get heard and fostering deeper self-belief in ability to create change

- Enhancing citizenship and political education, including knowledge of children's rights, structures and services

- Increasing independence and responsibility for actions

- Increasing ownership and care for services

- Improving sense of community and belonging.

The starting point in developing such a participatory research culture is to creatively and respectfully listen to young children.

What is creative listening?

In the Reggio Emilia early childhood centres of Northern Italy children are understood as being creative, intelligent and competent. The children are understood to have multiple modes of expression, including words, movement, drawing, painting, sculpture, shadow play, collage and music (Edwards et al., 1998). These diverse modes of creative expression are known as their 'hundred languages'.

The 'Hundred Languages' poem beautifully sums up this approach:

No Way. The Hundred is There
(from *The Hundred Languages of Children*)

The child
is made of one hundred.
The child has
a hundred languages
a hundred hands
a hundred thoughts
a hundred ways of thinking
of playing, of speaking.
A hundred always a hundred
ways of listening
of marvelling, of loving
a hundred joys
for singing and understanding
a hundred worlds
to discover
a hundred worlds to invent
a hundred worlds
to dream. The child has
a hundred languages
(and a hundred hundred hundred more)
but they steal ninety-nine.
The school and the culture
separate the head from the body.
They tell the child:
to think without hands
to do without head
to listen and not to speak
to understand without joy
to love and to marvel
only at Easter and Christmas.
They tell the child:
to discover the world already there
and of the hundred
they steal ninety-nine.
They tell the child:
that work and play
reality and fantasy
science and imagination
sky and earth
reason and dream

are things
that do not belong together
and thus they tell the child
that the hundred is not there.
The child says:
No way. The hundred *is* there.

(Loris Malaguzzi © 1996 Municipality of Reggio Emilia, Publishers Reggio Children; English trans. © Lella Gandini, 1983, in Edwards, Gandini and Forman, 1995, Ablex/ Greenwood Publishing Group.)

The poem is significant for early childhood researchers and practitioners since it reminds us that listening to young children need not be limited to the spoken word. Through their emphasis on the creative arts, the Reggio Emilia centres challenge the idea that visual forms of communication are somehow inferior to linguistic communication. Pressure is often put upon children to express themselves verbally, when young children might not yet have the experiences or vocabulary to do this. Young children competently express themselves through their play and through drawings and paintings and other expressive media. Emphasising visual forms of communication potentially empowers children who are pre-verbal, have language delay or have English as a second language (Lancaster and Broadbent, 2010). Hence, listening to the 'voice of the child' needs to be a process which is open to the many creative ways children express their views and experiences.

The National Children's Bureau (Dickins, 2004: 1) have creativity at the centre of their definition of 'listening': Listening is …

- an active process of receiving, interpreting and responding to communication. It includes all the senses and emotions and is not limited to the spoken word

- a necessary stage in ensuring the participation of all children

- an ongoing part of tuning in to all children as individuals in their everyday lives

- sometimes part of a specific consultation about a particular entitlement, choice, event or opportunity.

Understanding listening in this way is key to providing an environment in which all children feel confident, safe and powerful, ensuring they have the time and space to express themselves in whatever form suits them.

At the heart of creative listening to children is a constant raising of adult expectations of young children's abilities to communicate and express their desires and interests. The 'one hundred languages' of children *are* present and are waiting to be heard by researchers. However, early childhood researchers have to be open to these many languages in order to be able to *hear* them.

As adult researchers learn to work together with children, they may become more aware of children's strengths and competencies, and their skills become apparent in clear and tangible ways. These experiences help to create a more favourable environment for dialogue and understanding. When children's participation in research takes place in an environment of mutual respect, it can lead to a change in attitudes and the roles and capabilities of children. This change can lead to greater creativity, new ideas and deeper understanding not only of the issues under investigation, but to important issues in their community (Mann and Laws, 2004: 3).

Sensitive and respectful researchers working in an inclusive and participatory way with young children constantly engage children in creative and innovatory ways. Such researchers are well positioned to hear children's one hundred languages. The Mosaic approach has been pioneered as an effective way of listening to children's creative responses to their environment.

The Mosaic approach

The Mosaic approach (Clark and Moss, 2005) is an integrated approach which combines the visual with the verbal. A diverse range of traditional and innovative listening techniques are placed together to gain young children's views and experiences of their early childhood setting. The information collected through using the Mosaic approach can be used to make changes to the nursery.

The 'documentation' or recording process comprises a range of evidence including: narrative observations; consultations with the child, his or her key worker and his or her parents; children's drawings; children's photographs and children's maps. These listening research techniques are participatory and inclusive, and the wide variety of triangulated evidence can be represented as a *mosaic* of evidence (Figure 7.1).

There are two stages in the Mosaic approach:

- Stage one: Children and adults gathering the documentation.
- Stage two: Piecing together information for dialogue, reflection and interpretation.

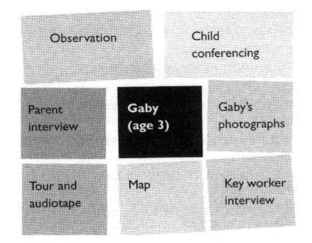

Figure 7.1   A mosaic of evidence

Combining the narratives and images of the individual pieces of the mosaic helps the researcher develop a good understanding of the children's priorities (Clark, 2005).

Throughout the Mosaic approach it is important that the children are involved in the interpretation of their photographs, drawings and tours. Within the Mosaic approach children are viewed as experts in their own lives, but they are not the only ones with this expertise. There is space within the Mosaic approach for a range of voices as well as the child's. 'What is advocated is that "another chair" be pulled up, alongside those already present around the decision-making tables: parents, carers, practitioners and policymakers. Service providers need to be joined by the children themselves' (Lancaster and Broadbent, 2010). Thus the Mosaic approach is a way of listening which acknowledges children and adults as co-constructors of meaning. The multi-method approach brings together children's own views with those of the family and staff.

Cameras and ethics

Taking their own photographs provides children with the possibilities of a powerful visual language. Children using cameras to take their own pictures of their nursery settings is a relatively recent research technique. Children know that photographs are enjoyable and are valued by adults, so children tend to enjoy taking photographs. Photographs are a powerful way for children to record aspects of their daily lives. Even very young children are quite capable of taking photographs of events and situations that affect them. These photographs can then be printed out and the pictures discussed with children.

Some early childhood institutions increasingly own digital cameras, computers and printing facilities. The advent of inexpensive digital cameras means that children can see their results instantaneously on the camera itself and the subsequent computer printouts. This fast process helps to focus children upon the pictures. If there is a delay of several days between taking the pictures and seeing the results, children's interest may have been lost and they may not be able to explain why they took the pictures. Disposable single-use cameras are also successful with young children because they are less expensive than digital cameras. They are also small and light enough for the children to walk around with and put in their pockets or bags to take with them.

If your research project involves you or the children taking *any* photographs within an early years setting, you *must* ensure that you have obtained permission from the manager, the practitioners, the parents and the children themselves. It is ethically critically important to inform all the stakeholders that the project might involve taking photographs. Parents and practitioners need to know *why* children are being given cameras and what will happen to the photographs. You must let the institution know how long you will keep the photographs and when you will destroy them. If you are going to take away any photographs for your project, make sure the children have a complete set of their photographs too. Hence, make two complete sets of photographs.

Sometimes institutions are willing to let you and the children take photographs as long as the photographs do not contain people's faces. Ethically it is important that if children are taking photographs of one another that they are told to ask other children if they are happy to have their pictures taken. Some children might not want to have their pictures taken.

Children's photographs and walking tours

A further inclusive participatory listening technique used in the Mosaic approach is the 'walking tour' (Clark and Moss, 2005). These visual walks offer children the opportunity to share their imaginative understandings of their environment. In some ways a walking tour is similar to an interview on the move. However, unlike some interviews, the child is in charge of the agenda and the geographical location. The walking tours can be done with individual children or in pairs and threes. At the end of the walking tour, children draw maps of their nursery onto which their photographs of important places are placed. Making maps together, using the children's drawings and photographs, is an inclusive participatory activity which can reveal valuable information about the children's perspectives of their institution.

A child's photographs of their day can be used as part of a child's and family's induction process. The new child is given a camera to take pictures of their daily routine in the nursery. They are asked to take photographs of what they like and dislike, the toys they play with, the areas of the room they use and the outside spaces. These photographs are placed in a book with the child's comments as to why they took the photographs. The book is shared with the parents, with the child explaining the photographs. Such a process of documenting and recording the child's day at nursery has proved successful with parents who are excited to see what their child does at nursery (Lancaster and Broadbent, 2010).

In addition to the children's perspectives gathered through the processes above, parents' and practitioners' perspectives can also be collected through the use of interviews. Parents and practitioners are extremely knowledgeable about the children and their views should be incorporated. Questions asked could include:

- What does your child enjoy doing at home?
- What do you think your child feels about being at the nursery?
- What does your child say at home about the nursery?
- What would be a good day for your child at the nursery?
- What do you think would be a bad day for your child at the nursery?

Sometimes the child's views echo the parents' and practitioners' and at other times there are differences of opinion. This range of evidence can be documented to provide an overview of a child's experiences at an early childhood setting.

Case study

A childminder wanted to find out more about Pam's perceptions of being in her house and then walking to the park. Pam was 3 years old. The child-minder explained to Pam that mummy and daddy wanted to know what Pam liked and disliked about her house and the walk to the park.

- What did Pam like and dislike about the house?
- What did she enjoy about going to the park and when she was in the park?

The childminder explained that together they would be sharing the photographs with Pam's parents. At first Pam was apprehensive about making a mistake with the camera but when the flash worked she knew that the picture had been taken. Her self-esteem and confidence visibly rose and she was soon happily taking photographs. Pam confidently led her childminder around the rooms she used and on the walk to the park showed her what she liked. Pam's comments were noted down as she took the photographs.

A visual tour by Pam (aged 3)

At the childminder's house

The childminder felt that Pam was in control of the visual tour and that she was positioned as the listener and learner. Giving Pam the camera

Figure 7.2 'I don't like the television 'cos it looks like an eye at me.'

Figure 7.3   'I like the books.'

Figure 7.4   'I like looking out of the window 'cos it's all out there.'

proved successful because Pam was often a quiet girl with her childminder. With the camera, however, Pam had been given a powerful means of visual expression and the camera proved a valuable way into Pam's thinking and understanding of her environment. As a consequence of the pictures, some changes were made around the house to accommodate Pam's

Figure 7.5   'I like those baskets 'cos they have my best toys in.'

Figure 7.6   'I don't like the shelf because I hit my head on the corner when I brush my teeth.'

expressions. The footstool was moved in the bathroom so she avoided the shelf; the television was turned around; and the childminder specifically looked for Ps in books and the environment. Until Pam had taken the photograph of the 'P' in the street, the childminder had not appreciated that Pam was so observant of such rich environmental print. Such small

Figure 7.7   'I can see a P. That's my name!'

Figure 7.8   'I like going on Daddy's bicycle.'

changes in Pam's daily routine may at first seem insignificant, but Pam's self-esteem was raised when she realised that the childminder was taking seriously what she had to say about her environment. Hence, Pam's expectations of being listened to were raised and the childminder's expectations of what Pam observed and how she could visually express herself were also

Figure 7.9 'I like to hide under here and my favourite colour is yellow.'

raised. Such raised expectations can lead to an enriched and more participatory relationship.

Pam was empowered by being able to take the pictures and make a book with them. It was with great delight that Pam shared her book with her parents. The above photographs were combined with the childminder's observations and the parent's comments about what their daughter liked. This conversation confirmed that Pam liked to hide in places, found great delight in finding Ps for her name and loved having books read to her. Pam's photographs and her perceptions were at the centre of the conversation which raised her self-esteem. The childminder was surprised at just how competent Pam was at using the digital camera. Pam's competence served as a useful reminder of how research techniques with young children need to work to children's strengths and abilities rather than their perceived weaknesses. From such small beginnings it is possible to see how young children's insightful comments may be used to inform changes to existing provision or to contribute to the new designs of buildings.

Children's drawings

Children's drawings can be seen as a child's attempts to make sense of their experiences on at least three levels: cognitive, affective and linguistic (Hawkins,

2002). Cognitively, drawing is thought in action and is a rich way of thinking, of knowing and of exploring the world 'out there' through the intellect and the senses. Affectively, drawing and painting are ways for children to explore and learn about their feelings. Linguistically, drawing and painting provide a space for children to develop their visual language. Drawing *is* young children's early writing and is seen as being as powerful as writing as a means of representation (Kress, 1997). In addition to the above benefits, drawing and painting are clearly vital to play, the imagination and creativity.

Many young children love to draw and paint, and will spend long periods of time concentrating upon their creations. Consequently, drawings and paintings are an excellent inclusive and participatory research technique with which to listen to children. Drawings are self-initiated and spontaneously made by some children, and hence using children's drawings lends itself to 'non-invasive, non-confrontational and participatory research' (Morrow and Richards, 1996: 100). If you are going to use children's drawings in your research you must gain informed assent from the children to do so (see Chapter 3). Drawings can be personal creations in which intimate and sometimes private experiences and knowledge are shared with familiar people by the children. The children may feel uncomfortable with you taking their pictures away for a wider audience than they were originally intended for by the child.

Children's interpretations of their pictures

A potential limitation of using children's drawings and paintings in your research study is that the researcher can all too easily impute to them their own interpretations. 'Consulting children by asking them to draw can gain illuminating evidence, but many drawings are ambiguous or vague sketches, and it is better to use them together with spoken or written comments from the child, explaining the picture' (Alderson, 2008: 200). Hence, if you are using children's drawings in your research project, it is imperative that the children are given the time and space to explain the meanings of their pictures and paintings. Researchers sometimes ask children to write a short story about their picture or to write a story and then illustrate it. However, with young children, some of whom do not yet formally write, discussing with the child what it is they are drawing *as they draw it*, can be invaluable. Sometimes a young child, when asked what their picture is of, might simply reply, 'a picture'. This may be because the meaning of the picture occurs during the actual *process* of drawing or painting itself.

Hence, once the picture has been completed the meaning is lost. In the following case study it can be seen that listening to children whilst they are actively engaged in the process of drawing or painting or model-making itself may provide a good insight into what the picture represents for the child. This is because

> what the child really wants to do is to talk to himself in pictures, which suggests that the child weaves stories around the marks being made, each scribble having particular meaning dictating the story's direction so that the whole turns into a fantastical journey, a parallel for active fantasy play. (Coates, 2002: 26)

In the following case study of the media, Jake re-creates a story in his drawing.

📁 Case study

The influence of the media on children's lives

The researcher used observations of play, the children's drawings and focused discussion with the children to collect her evidence with six nursery children. The researcher wanted to know what sort of games the children played and how these games were influenced by children's television and video stories. Specifically in her observations the researcher listened for any television language and songs used; if any television characters were adopted during role play and how the play narratives were constructed.

In addition to observations, the children were also asked to draw pictures at nursery and at home, particularly after they had been watching television. The researcher asked the children if the tape recorder could be kept on *whilst* they drew their drawings. The following is a transcript of Jake talking while drawing a picture he made after watching the television show *Brum and the Naughty Dog* in which a naughty dog gets stuck down a deep hole.

As Jake drew his picture he made the following rich, detailed comments concerning his drawing:

> *Jake, drawing and talking*: The dog's dug an either further one ... There's a tunnel here and it goes down here and there's another one here. And down here is a rabbit.
> *Researcher*: What's the rabbit doing?
> *Jake, drawing and talking*: There's a mole here ...
> *Researcher*: These are all underground creatures aren't they ...

Figure 7.10   Jake's picture

Jake, drawing and talking: But the dog isn't … the dog dug this really massive hole.
Researcher: Why?
Jake, drawing and talking: 'Cos he wanted to … he was getting his bones. The mole thought the dog wanted a bone so then the mole pushed a bone down the tunnel and it came out there and the dog could eat it. The mole found lots of bones and he gave them all to the dog … he got lots and lots and lots of bones. And last of all the massive bone and that

was Clifford's bone. And last of all one of Clifford's other big bones but Clifford's already eaten a bit. He's got loads of fat bones, they look like bums!!!

Last of all the longest and thinnest Clifford's been eaten through some of them ...

And there was a bone that was so big it couldn't even fit through ...

And last of all but not least an even bigger bone ...

The mole keeps giving him bones look here's one coming down the tunnel into his mouth ... and then he catches it.

Jake is clearly active in his reinterpretation of the video. The initial media plot has been creatively reworked and developed by the child in his 'storying' around the drawing. In places the language is reflective of his book language, 'and last of all' which is said several times over. Interestingly, Jake has also used Clifford, another children's television dog character, in his intertextual story of his drawing. The rich, detailed, creative and vivid language used during the dynamic process of the drawing itself can be counterposed with the sometimes stilted, laborious and short descriptions which can occur when an adult asks the child what it is a picture of.

In the following case study Sarah, who used observations and focus group conversations, also used drawings to find out more about what children understand by friends.

🗀 Case study

Sarah wanted to know more about the relationship between friendships and gender. How does gender affect friendships in early childhood? One of the techniques she used was to ask the children to draw pictures of their friends and to write down next to their pictures why they chose these people as their friends.

As John and Peter, Year 1 boys, told Sarah about their friendships they drew the picture (Figure 7.11) together. John did the drawings and Peter wrote the children's names. The drawings helped the boys to focus upon the conversation. As they drew the pictures they discussed why they liked having the children as friends.

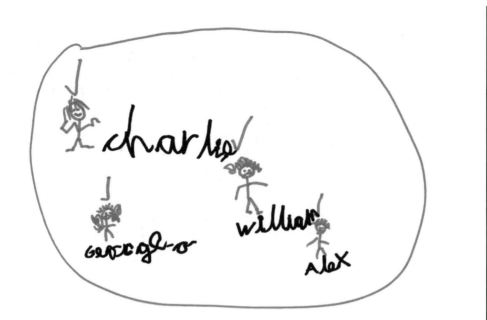

Figure 7.11   John and Peter's picture

Sarah: I want you to draw pictures of your friends and tell me why you like them. Only draw the people that are your special friends since it wouldn't be nice to draw people you don't like. Is it okay to tape-record this conversation as you draw? We can listen to the tape afterwards and you tell me if what you have said is okay to write down. What do you think?

John: Yes it's okay.

Peter: Yes just the children we like to play with.

John: Charlie's got quite long hair hasn't he so it goes like this.

Peter: We like playing with Charlie because he loves rockets and I like them too.

John: And they blast off really really fast. We go like this ...
John gets up from the table and pretends to be a rocket 'blasting off' making rocket noises.

John: I'm gonna draw someone else now. This is William because we love racing and I'm always second and we raced in our teams and my team came second.

Peter: Friends are fun and we love racing with them! William loves racing with us.

Sarah: Who else is your friend?

John: George is and he has long hair like this. Look that's what he's like. I like George because he plays with knight things and swords and everything and they can chop the houses down. He's got wooden ones at home which he carved with his Daddy he said. I've played with them and we went clash clash and one time he flicked mine so hard that it got stuck in the tree.

Peter: I like Alex because he plays with lots of soft toys and he brings them for Show and Tell and when it's Golden Time we can play with them in the classroom. He brings in his penguins and a big hippopotamus and because I'm a friend I can play with them. That's why we're friends.

Sarah: How do you choose your friends?

John: I run up to them and I say can I play with you and they say and I say what are you playing and then I ask them whose game is it and then they say yes or no. If they say no I go and play with someone else but if they say yes then I join in the game.

Sarah: Do you play with girls at all?

Peter: No. Because they scream a lot. They chase each other and scream a lot and it makes my ears blocked.

Sarah: Do any of the girls play with you?

Peter: Most of the boys play with the boys and the girls play with the girls. Camille and Molly play with the boys though and they are in the same class.

The drawings provided a powerful focus for the conversation. The drawings and conversation, Sarah's observations and the teacher's observations confirmed the gendered pattern of relationships within the Year 1 class. Sarah shared her research findings with the teacher and together they discussed ways to challenge the stereotypes boys held about girls and vice versa. In this way it can be seen that listening to the boys' conversations and their drawings encouraged curriculum development and thinking.

Summary

This chapter has discussed:

- the ways in which creative listening and participation can empower children

- the Mosaic approach of creatively listening to young children

- the possibilities of children being co-researchers, setting the research agenda and collecting and interpreting the evidence

- the importance of children interpreting their own drawings and photographs.

Recommended reading 📖

Clark, A. and Moss, P. (2005) *Spaces to Play: More Listening to Young Children Using the Mosaic Approach*. London: National Children's Bureau.
This book explores the different ways in which young children can be listened to regarding their outdoor environments. The book provides thorough and detailed research advice and possibilities for incorporating the multiple voices of young children.

Lancaster, Y. and Broadbent, V. (2010) *Listening to Young Children*, 2nd edn. Maidenhead: Coram Family and Open University Press.
This book is a comprehensive resource to support practitioners in understanding what it means to listen and respond to what young children have to say. The book provides many examples of creative ways of listening to young children that can be used as creative research data collecting methods for your early childhood research project.

8

Interviewing
children
and adults

Learning objectives

This chapter will help you to:

- understand the different ways of consulting with children and adults
- become aware of the ethical considerations when consulting and using questionnaires
- practise using a tape recorder for recording consultations
- understand the ways in which consultations and questionnaires can be used together.

Different types of interviews

Structured interviews are quite similar to questionnaires in that the interviewer has a set of predetermined questions which he/she asks in a set order. This set of predetermined fixed questions, known as the interview schedule, determines and dominates the structure of the interview (Denscombe, 2007).

In the semi-structured interview and unstructured interview the focus is shifted away from the researcher with the fixed interview schedule and towards the issues and interests of the research participant. The role of the interviewer is one of facilitator and enabler who encourages the research participant to 'speak their mind' on issues. The interviewer 'gets the ball rolling' and thereafter listens carefully, asking for development of issues as they arise during the conversation. Where necessary the interviewer will ask a direct question but the direction and content of the conversation stems from the research participant. Semi-structured and unstructured interviews are on a continuum, and an interview will slide back and forth between them. In a semi-structured or unstructured interview there is more space for the research participant to elaborate on points which are important to him/her.

The interview guide

During semi-structured interviews the researcher usually has an interview guide which simply lists the points which the researcher wants to cover but, unlike the interview schedule, the guide is not fixed and predetermined. The interview guide is simply five or six open-ended questions to guide the interview rather than dictate the structure and content. Such an open-ended research guide allows the researcher to keep the interview focused upon the research subject and at the same time be sufficiently flexible to allow for the interview to change direction if the respondent wants the discussion to go in a different direction. The following is Sarah's interview guide concerning friendship with a group of children:

- How do you make friends with other people?
- What sort of people do you choose to be your friend?
- What makes a good friend?
- What sort of things do you like best about your friends?

- What makes a bad friend?

- What sort of things do bad friends do?

Activity

Now try writing an interview guide for your research topic. Remember to base such a guide upon the literature, your feelings and your observations of the research setting. Pilot this interview guide with your friends/family/children to see how it works. Have you left out any important questions or avenues for discussion?

Probing

An important skill that interviewers need to develop is the ability to know how and when to probe the research participant for more information. Such probing helps to elaborate, confirm and clarify what the research participant is saying. Such probing often requires that the researcher is familiar with the issues being discussed and is aware of what is important and needs further clarification. This is where your background reading and research about the setting are important.

Probing type questions can include the following:

- I don't quite understand, can you explain a bit more?

- Can you give me an example of what you have just said?

- What do you mean?

- Can you give me more details about that?

In your pilot interview with your friends and family make sure you use some probing-type questions. Can you think of any more?

The differences between an interview and a chat

Despite the fact that interviewing is based upon a skill that researchers already possess, that is, the ability to hold a conversation, good research interviewing is much more demanding than it might at first appear.

- The issue of informed consent (see Chapter 3) places a responsibility upon you. You have a responsibility to tell the respondent to stop if they begin to share material which may force the researcher to break confidentiality due to child protection issues.

- Knowledge of the subject, gained from a thorough literature review and knowledge of your specific research setting, gained from OFSTED websites, walking around the area and noting its sociocultural environment, and general reading about the geographical location and its history, all contribute to your knowledge of the setting and help to produce a more focused and informed discussion.

- Empathy, respect and sensitivity for the research participants are essential to a good interview. You need the ability to 'read' the social dynamics not just the content. If the respondent shows signs of feeling uncomfortable with an issue, you need to move on.

- You need to remain non-judgemental during the interview. Researchers sometimes hold strong opinions about the subject and the respondents' viewpoints might be different. Your job is to respectfully listen to the respondents' viewpoints, not try to persuade them of your feelings about the topic!

In the following interview guides about gender, can you see how the first interview guide is prejudiced and will lead the children to think in certain ways?

Interview 1

Are your best friends boys or girls? Why?
Why do girls like reading and writing and boys like playing football?
Why do girls play quietly and boys play noisily?
Why do girls like dolls and boys like guns?

In this first interview guide the questions are not neutral and objective but rather prejudiced and stereotypical. The questions are *leading* the children along a certain train of thought. The questions confirm stereotypes and invite the children to expand upon such stereotypical notions. The prejudices will be picked up by the children and other stereotypical examples found. The children may wish to challenge such stereotyped notions but the questions are so biased that the children may feel unable to do so.

Interview 2

Can you tell me what you think about girls and boys?
Are girls and boys the same?

What do you think about boys?
What do you think about girls?
What did you think about the video?

In this second interview guide the questions are much more open-ended and neutral. They are not leading questions but rather allow for a range of possible answers. The questions are sufficiently open to allow for responses which challenge gender stereotypes.

Focus group conversations with children

Interviews with adults often involve one-to-one interviewing. Focusing and listening to one person's viewpoints makes the interview relatively easy to manage. One-to-one interviews are fairly easily arranged and are a good way into interviewing for the novice researcher. However, children can feel threatened and intimidated by a one-to-one interview with a researcher, especially if the children are not familiar with that researcher. Being familiar with the children you hope to interview or consult with is critically important to the success of the interview. Such relationships are important when interviewing children because they are not used to their opinions and experiences being sought by unknown adults (Folque, 2010). To this end many researchers spend a week or two working voluntarily and making observations in the setting. During this period the researcher gets to know the children and, hopefully, builds up the children's trust. For example, Sarah arranged a two-week block voluntarily working with and observing the children before she interviewed them, and this gave her the time to develop relationships with children.

However, it is important to choose the group of children carefully because some children might dominate others and shy children might not talk for fear of reprisal or ridicule when they do. Here again, the choice of children for a focus group discussion critically depends upon the researcher's familiarity with the children. Hence, often the key worker or teacher can help the researcher choose which children to put into a focus group. He or she will have a good knowledge of which children will work best together.

Central to the success that can be gained from group conversations is the potential for the power dynamics between the researcher and the children to be shifted in favour of the children (Folque, 2010). Thus, group interviews where a small group of friends – perhaps three or four – are interviewed together tends to make children more relaxed and comfortable. Children tend to enjoy social situations and activities; hence focus groups with other children appeal to their sociability. Moreover, children can listen to each other's ideas in focus groups and encourage each other in the process of articulating their thoughts. In mixed-age groups younger children can gain encouragement to talk from the older children. Therefore, focus groups tend to be successful in terms of generating discussion amongst the children. In successful focus groups the researcher can take on the role of discussion facilitator rather than being 'the interviewer' with a set of specific questions.

> Children talking together replicates the small group setting that they are familiar with in the classroom where conversation seems to flow effortlessly. Children aged six or less are difficult to interview alone and they find it hard to respond to direct questions about themselves … Small group discussions allow children to set their own agendas and the research topic to be woven into children's talk about their daily lives and social worlds. (Mauthner, 1997: 26)

Thus in Connolly's (1998) research on 5- and 6-year-olds' identity construction in an inner city primary school, he found that once a question had been asked, the children would take control of the discussion. Connolly (1998: 8) states that:

> the interviews were usually held in a separate room in the school and generally involved three children. Usually a child was picked (from those who said they wished to participate) from a class and asked to nominate two others whom they wished to come along and who wanted to participate themselves. The interviews were largely unstructured, with the children being given the space to articulate their own experiences and concerns. My role was simply one of *facilitator*, in that I would ask very general questions concerning what they did in the playground that day or what they liked to do at home. This would usually be enough for the children to develop their own lines of enquiry and discussion among themselves. My interventions following that were largely confined to encouraging the children to elaborate on what they had just said.

Connolly spent several months observing and listening to the children in the school before carrying out focused interviews. This familiarity with the children may have been partially responsible for the way in which the children talked so freely and openly with him.

Lancaster and Broadbent (2010) provide a useful overview of the strengths and limitations of focus group conversations.

Strengths:

- An appropriate technique for 5–6-year-olds especially when children know or like each other

- Provides an opportunity to work collaboratively – encourages interaction between children

- Can be empowering for individuals by building confidence

- Groups can give children space to raise issues that they want to discuss

- Recognises children as experts in their own settings

- Insights can be gained into young children's shared understandings of everyday life

- Generates new ideas through the interactions between all members of the group

- It is about having conversations rather than question and answer interviews

- Familiar to children.

Limitations:

- Difficult to identify individual from group view

- Individuals can be influenced by others in a group situation.

Children as researchers

The power dynamics between adults and children is perhaps the major difficulty that faces researchers. Morrow and Richards (1996: 98) note, 'The biggest ethical challenge for researchers working with children is the disparities in power and status between adults and children'. Such power dynamics can be a barrier to the collection of high-quality evidence from young children. A possible way to overcome this difficulty is to invite other children to be researchers themselves. Thus children interview other children. This 'child-to-child' technique has been pioneered in international development as a tool for conveying information to children as well as to discover their views (Gibbs et al., 2002). The thinking behind this method is that children, because of their 'inside knowledge', might be able to ask more relevant questions than adults. Older children can work with younger children to elicit their views. The closeness in age helps to alleviate some of the power differentials and the older children's interests, perceptions and understandings might be that much closer to the younger children than the best attempts by adults could ever be. In the following case study older children were co-researchers and made a video for younger children to help them settle into Reception class. The case study shows that the research had real and unanticipated outcomes.

Case study

Debbie was interested in involving Year 1 children as co-researchers in a project. She explained that research was concerned with finding out more about things. She showed the children a range of methods to collect people's views of things, including asking people about issues using a tape recorder and videoing events. The children practised using tape recorders to record conversations and also practised making videos of their favourite things in the classroom.

Debbie invited a group of children to work with her on a project of the children's own choosing. The children suggested several projects which they wished to research including:

- litter
- things they liked and disliked about the school
- being helpful and kind to others
- setting up a school sweet shop.

Debbie gave the children time to discuss the different topics amongst themselves, make drawings and develop their ideas. The main issues which came out of these discussions were concerning things the children liked and disliked about the school. Figure 8.1 shows Sam's picture of things he likes and dislikes about school.

Figure 8.1   Sam's picture

The first picture shows Rainbow class "cos that's where you do loads of art and art is really good'; the second picture shows 'the big grassy field where we can play and run around lots'; the third picture shows 'eating a nice lunch with corn and sausages'; the fourth picture shows 'the really bad thing, teachers shouting. Lots of people shout when they're cross and it makes my ears hurt in the class'. The fifth picture shows how good and bad children's names are written on the board and 'my name is never written on board for either'. The sixth picture shows 'Golden Time' which is great "cos we play for a long time'.

Debbie gave the children time to discuss different topics amongst them-selves, make drawings and develop their ideas. With Debbie's support it was decided to combine two topics: things we like and do not like, and being helpful and kind to others. Some of the children talked about how they had younger siblings and friends in the nursery attached to the primary school and the children wanted to help these younger children settle into the Reception class in the following term. This was thought to be a good idea and, in particular, it was decided to show them the things they might really enjoy – such as the big grassy field; 'Golden Time' for playing; doing art and the lunches. The children thought they should not tell the nursery children about the shouting because it might scare them. However, Debbie noted the children's concerns about teachers shouting.

The Year 1 children decided that the best way to show the young children what the Big School was like was to make a video of important things. Debbie suggested that they did not yet know what was important for the younger children. So the children decided that they would go and talk to the younger children about the things they wanted to know more about in joining the Big School. When they knew what the younger children wanted to know they would make a 'helpful and kind video'.

The Year 1 children and Debbie visited the nursery children and told them that they wanted to help them settle into Reception class next term. Some of the nursery children did not wish to participate in the project but the children who had older siblings as Year 1 researchers were keen to join in. In pairs the older children asked groups of younger children what they knew about the Big School and what scared them. The Year 1 children used tape recorders to record the conversations.

Upon return to their classroom, the Year 1 children listened to the tapes and, together with Debbie, identified the following themes which the younger children wanted to know more about. The main issues which came out of these discussions were:

- Where were the toilets?
- What friends would there be?

- Where did children eat and what food was there?
- What did people do at playtime?
- Will the older children hurt me?

In groups of three the children used the digital video camera to film where the toilets were located; that you had to ask for school dinners or packed lunch at register time; that you had to line up for dinner or sit at tables for packed lunch; that you could play on the big grassy field when it was not raining or the hard playground when it was wet, and they filmed different games that were played in the playground. The video also showed that if you did not have a friend you could ask the dinner ladies for help. The children talked about 'some nasty big children who hurt people'. Debbie realised that the school did not have an anti-bullying policy. Debbie promised the children that she would look into this and let the children know what the school's response was. (Subsequently the school did write an anti-bullying policy.)

With the children, Debbie edited the video on the computer and the children took it to the nursery to show it to the nursery children. The nursery children were delighted to see the video and it led to a lot more questions being asked which the Year 1 children were happy to answer.

The above project was successful because Debbie played the role of facilitator of the research and the children were the co-researchers. The children were the initiators of the ideas, collected the evidence and produced a video to help the nursery children. Producing the video showed the children that their ideas and the knowledge they had generated were important. Debbie reported that the Year 1 children's self-confidence and self-esteem had visibly risen as a result of making the video. The fact that the school had listened to and taken on board the children's concerns around bullying in the playground, and had subsequently acted to produce an anti-bullying policy, had further enhanced the children's self-confidence. The video the Year 1 children made concerned toilets, lunch and playing on the grass. The development of the anti-bullying policy represents a significant step towards acting upon children's interests and concerns. Perhaps sometime in the near future Sam's frustration with 'teachers shouting' might also be addressed. It is important to remember that young children's increased participation in their institutions, through such a research project as described above, is a process. Working with children as fellow researchers is a major step in the direction of participatory and inclusive research with young children.

Using structured activities

When interviewing children, some researchers have found it best to do so whilst the children are actually engaged in an activity. 'Structured activities can be effectively integrated into group discussions and interviews in order to provide a focus for children' (Mauthner, 1997: 26).

Through the use of books, prompts, games, puppets, soft toys and Personna Dolls (Browne, 1998) researchers can choose to engage in a gentle child-centred discussion with the children. Using children's drawings and their photographs encourages the interview to be child-centred and focused. Using children's drawings and photographs in the process of listening to children is discussed in the following chapter. Using child-centred structured activities helps to avoid 'the high-control, adult-dominated and question and answer format' (Brooker, 2001: 166) which some interviews can become. Through the use of participatory research techniques the researcher respectfully attempts to enter the world with which the child is familiar. Such socially inclusive ways of working with the children encourage high-quality and valid research interviews. Indeed, Brooker (2001) states that if children do not engage in valid discussion with the researcher, the fault lies with the researcher.

Reflective interviewing

Initially Sarah chose Circle Time to talk with the children about friendships because the children were familiar with Circle Time. Circle Time involved all the children who had chosen to take part in the research, sitting in a circle and passing a teddy bear around to each other. Each child got a chance to talk only when he or she was holding the teddy bear. Sarah explained:

> Circle Time worked really well because the children were used to doing this and talking about sensitive issues such as bullying. At the beginning I told the children to talk about the qualities of friendship and not to say who the children's actual friends were since it may be hurtful if a child's name was not mentioned by someone they thought was their friend. The children were really good at this because it sort of fitted in with what the children were used to and had already been doing. They knew the ground rules for Circle Time and how to talk about sensitive issues. They passed a teddy bear around and when holding it they said what they thought friendship qualities were about. Equally if they chose not to say anything

they just passed the teddy to the next person. Some children chose to do this. But it was still a school-type situation and I felt with some children that they were giving me the 'correct' answers. This may have been because the teacher sat with us and I feel that her presence affected what some of the children said and did not say.

Sarah's comments above show her sensitive reflection on the Circle Time situation. Sarah reflected upon how some children were supplying answers which they felt fitted in with what the teacher expected from them – thereby fulfilling the perceived expectations of the teacher. During Circle Time Sarah realised that 'test questioning' was occuring where the children were expected to produce the 'correct' response for her and the teacher.

Children are used from an early age to adults asking them questions *to which the adults clearly know the answers already.* In other words, children learn that much of adult questioning is 'test' questioning – 'I know the answer, but let's see if you know' – to which there are right or wrong answers. Hence, in order to produce the required response, much of the children's effort consists in working out what is in the adult's mind. (Brooker, 2001: 167)

Consequently, Sarah interviewed small groups of three and four children, and sat on the carpet with them. Sitting on the carpeted floor in the cosy book corner and out of earshot of the teacher provided a more convivial context for the children to talk. She started by reading the children *Something Else* and encouraged the children to think about how Something made friends with Something Else. On another occasion she used the class teddy bear, pretending that he was new to the class and wanted to make friends with the children. What sort of things should teddy do to make friends in the classroom? The discussion was further personalised by encouraging the children to bring in their favourite teddy bears and soft animals and talk about how they would make friends if they were new to the classroom.

With each interview Sarah situated herself as an 'inexpert' about friendships, particularly about friendships between children because she was not a child. She stated that she did not know very much about children at all but was very interested in them and wanted to learn all she could about children and friendships. Being familiar with the children, reading with the children, playing games with soft toys and positioning herself as an inexpert all encouraged the children to talk.

Sarah read *Something Else* and discussed it with the children. The children then 'introduced' their soft toys and said how they made friends with other toys. Once the children had begun to talk freely and with confidence about friendship, Sarah asked the children about their friendships in school.

Sarah:	I want to know more about your friendships. I don't really know anything about how children make friendships. Can you help me please by telling me what things makes a good friend?
Jake:	I like a friend that is kind to me and helps me with my work and I like a friend that plays football with me. All the boys play football, Jake, Lewis …
Lewis:	Yeah, yeah I like a friend that plays football with me and plays with me in the playground.
Jane:	I like a friend that plays with me. I like it when my friends come to my house for a party.
Lewis:	Yeah, yeah … I like a friend that comes to my house and plays with my remote control car.
Sarah:	Good for you! You are so clever at making friends. I bet you have so many friends. Thank you for telling me all that. I'm beginning to learn about how to make friends now. You're just great. Now listen can you tell me the sort of things that you don't like friends to do?
Jane:	I don't like a friend who puts me down or is mean to me. I don't like a friend that bosses me about.
Jake:	I don't like a friend that hits me. You have to tell before they run to the teacher and tell a lie! Tell them that you hit them!!! I don't like people who do that.
Lewis:	Billy isn't my friend when he loses a game. He always loses and hits other people and then … and then hits me too.

A wide diversity of children

It is critically important to ensure that you have interviewed as wide a variety of the children in the setting as possible. Hence boys and girls and ethnic minority children and disabled children should be represented in your sample of children (Booth and Ainscow, 2004). Hearing this diversity of children's 'voices' adds to the validity of your research by ensuring that no one voice, for example, boys' or girls', dominate the evidence you generate. It is important to remember that children do not form a homogeneous group but, rather, that children's voices are many and varied. This can depend upon the child's gender, class, ethnicity, mother tongue, location and physical ability. A seemingly similar group such as black boys will have marked differences in their life experiences dependent upon their ethnicity, class, geographical location, physical ability or disability (Sewell, 1998). Your research should attempt to reflect this rich diversity of children's experiences and opinions, and in this way your research will prove all the more convincing to the reader.

Tape-recording

Tape-recording, rather than writing the interview down, is an important research interview habit to develop because it allows you to do your main job, that is, active *listening*. Tape-recording allows you the space and time to focus upon the discussion with the research participant (Denscombe, 2007). Not writing everything down, which is almost impossible anyway, frees you up to concentrate and think about the issues arising in the interview. The interview may go in different directions than you expect, and you need to focus upon the content and asking appropriate questions rather than your handwriting.

Occasionally a person may not wish the interview to be tape-recorded, usually because they are unsure of what you will do with the tape. This situation might arise where the interviewer and the research participant do not know each other. You must inform the research participants as to what you intend to do with the tape (see Chapter 3 on informed consent). Children tend to enjoy hearing their voices on the tape recorder and will gladly sit and listen to the tape with you. This provides a good opportunity to check with the children the meaning of the conversation and to clarify points you may be unclear about. This adds to the validity of the evidence you collect.

Always check that you are completely familiar with the working of the tape recorder and that you have sufficient tapes and recording time. There is nothing more frustrating than finding that the interview you carefully set up was not recorded because the tape needed turning over or the batteries ran out.

Transcribing tapes, or writing them up, takes a long time. A half-hour of tape-recorded interview can take two hours to transcribe. It is best to play the whole tape through and listen carefully to the ideas and themes arising in the interview and note these down. Once you have an overall understanding of the whole tape, it is much easier to replay it and select exactly what you need from the interview. This process of listening and re-listening to the tape, and transcribing key parts word for word, gives a level of understanding and analysis that is difficult to achieve with jotted down notes. With the tape recorder you get *everything* that was said and with its transcription you will be able to carry out a thorough and reflective analysis.

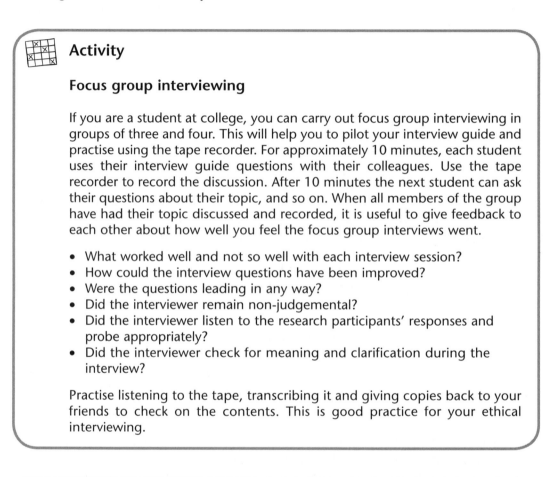

Activity

Focus group interviewing

If you are a student at college, you can carry out focus group interviewing in groups of three and four. This will help you to pilot your interview guide and practise using the tape recorder. For approximately 10 minutes, each student uses their interview guide questions with their colleagues. Use the tape recorder to record the discussion. After 10 minutes the next student can ask their questions about their topic, and so on. When all members of the group have had their topic discussed and recorded, it is useful to give feedback to each other about how well you feel the focus group interviews went.

- What worked well and not so well with each interview session?
- How could the interview questions have been improved?
- Were the questions leading in any way?
- Did the interviewer remain non-judgemental?
- Did the interviewer listen to the research participants' responses and probe appropriately?
- Did the interviewer check for meaning and clarification during the interview?

Practise listening to the tape, transcribing it and giving copies back to your friends to check on the contents. This is good practice for your ethical interviewing.

Summary

This chapter has discussed:

- a range of different types of interviews with children and adults

- the skills and sensitivity needed to carry out focus group discussions with young children

- ways in which children can act as co-researchers
- the ways in which structured activities can be used with young children whilst interviewing
- the importance of tape-recording interviews wherever possible.

Recommended reading 📖

Folque, M. (2010) 'Interviewing young children', in G. MacNaughton, S. Rolfe and I. Siraj-Blatchford (eds) *Doing Early Childhood Research: International Perspectives on Theory and Practice*, 2nd edn. Buckingham: Open University Press. This thorough chapter contains a wealth of information on how to carry out ethically sound interviews with young children. It also details the ways in which the sampling process can occur through the description of a case study.

Denscombe, M. (2007) *The Good Research Guide*. Maidenhead: Open University Press.
Chapter 10 provides the novice researcher with a full run-down of the necessary practicalities involved in interviewing.

9

Writing and using questionnaires

Learning objectives

This chapter will help you to:

- develop an awareness of how and when to use questionnaires
- understand the possibilities and limitations of using questionnaires
- write questionnaires
- evaluate some examples of questionnaires.

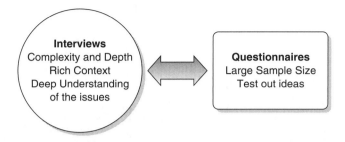

Figure 9.1   Interviews and questionnaires are complementary when used together

Questionnaires can be used for a wide variety of reasons in small-scale research projects. If you wish to survey a relatively large group of people to find out their attitudes and knowledge, then questionnaires can be a useful and relatively cheap method of rapidly collecting a wide range of views. Unlike in-depth interviewing, questionnaires tend to provide the *broad* picture of people's experiences and views. Questionnaires work through the use of standard questions which make it possible to draw comparisons between responses. Questionnaires which are sent by post or by email involve little or no personal interaction and hence can encourage frankness of response due to the anonymity afforded. However, the contradictory, ambiguous and rich detail so often elicited during interviews is unlikely to be gained using questionnaires. So it is best to use both questionnaires and interviews and other forms of data collection together.

As with all research methods, you must consider *why* you wish to use questionnaires. Questionnaires can only ever provide part of the answer to your overall research questions. Questionnaires need to be used in conjunction with other research methods such as interviews, drawings and observations.

In Figure 9.1, the interviews add the 'flesh' to the 'bones' provided by the questionnaire survey. Pilot interviews can be used to gain more detailed information about the subject. The material from the pilot interviews can be used to feed into pilot questionnaires and thereafter the questionnaires. In this manner considerable knowledge can be built up before questionnaires are printed and sent out. In addition, the results of questionnaires sometimes raise more questions than answers for both the respondent and the researcher. Some respondents write lengthy replies to questions and would be happy to talk further at length with the researcher about the issues. Therefore, some questionnaires ask for the respondent's telephone number so if he/she wishes to be contacted again by

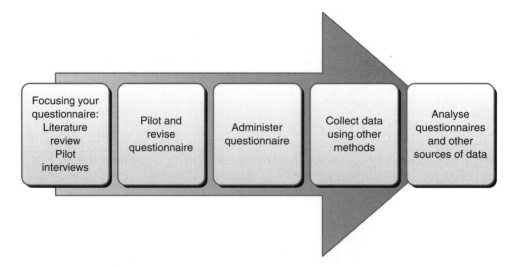

Figure 9.2 The steps in carrying out a small-scale questionnaire survey

the researcher they can do so. In this way it is possible to follow up some interesting questionnaire responses with further in-depth interviewing to further elicit views.

Three ways to administer your questionnaires

1. *Self-completion questionnaire.* This is a good technique to collect a relatively high number of questionnaires. It is possible to either hand out the questionnaires yourself to the respondents or it can be posted or emailed out to the respondents. It is important that the self-completion questionnaire is relatively simple and straightforward so that the respondents can understand what is required of them for successful completion. Of course it is also possible to phone or text the respondents and let them know that the questionnaire will be coming via email.

2. *Face-to-face questionnaire.* Here the researcher has the respondent with them and goes through the questionnaire. After completing the questionnaire it is possible to probe some of the responses more deeply. Face-to-face questionnaires are useful for several reasons: they ensure the questionnaire is successfully completed; they can be used with children and adults who are unable to read; and they allow the researcher to probe.

3. *Telephone questionnaires*. This is relatively expensive and time consuming. It also depends upon the good will of the respondent having the time to complete the questionnaire over the phone, often while they are at work. It also takes considerable skill to listen to the respondent and write down their response to open-ended questions. It is possible to use this technique in order to follow up a questionnaire that has been either sent out in the post or via email. To save the respondent time, the questionnaire can be completed over the phone.

Ethical issues and questionnaires

The issues concerning informed consent discussed in Chapter 3 are applicable if you are using questionnaires. As part of your ethical responsibilities you must gain informed consent from the appropriate gatekeepers, such as headteachers and nursery managers. It may be important for the respondents to know that their questionnaires will be anonymous – they might then give more honest responses. Self-completion questionnaires can clearly only be used by literate older children and adults. Booth and Ainscow (2004: 29) suggest that, with young children, questionnaires should only be used as prompts for conversations with children. Furthermore even with older children, researchers cannot assume that young people will attach the same understanding to questions used. Where possible, child-led vocabulary is advisable, with careful attention given to the layout of the questionnaire (National Children's Bureau, 2002).

Activity

What are your research questions?
What sort of – and how much – information do you need to answer your research questions?
What does a questionnaire add to your research study?
How can you justify using a questionnaire?
What will you learn about your research topic by using questionnaires?
What other research methods will you use? Why?

In the following case study Lucy discusses *why* she chooses to use questionnaires with the professionals in her sample. Her questionnaire sample was not made up of a random selection of participants but, rather, was 'purposive' sampling

(Denscombe, 2007). Through the use of her personal contacts and by reading OFSTED websites, she 'handpicked' the institutions and contacted the people she wished to survey. She sent out her questionnaire to 70 potential respondents.

Case study

As you read this case study, list all the things which Lucy did *before* she sent out her questionnaires.

Lucy's research on domestic violence was centrally concerned with a comparison of attitudes between the different professionals: teachers, nursery workers, social workers and domestic violence officers. She wanted to compare their attitudes on whether they felt schools should educate children about domestic violence. She wanted to gain an overall impression as to each profession's feelings in this area. Lucy felt that a questionnaire survey was suited to revealing the general feelings of each profession. Lucy decided to follow up some of the questionnaires with one-to-one interviews to clarify and further discuss issues emerging from the generalised questionnaire responses.

After reading widely in the area and informally discussing the issues with friends and colleagues, Lucy piloted her questionnaire with her friends and colleagues at college. Her 'critical friends' were helpful in providing comments. It was important that, before she spent money on photocopying and stamps and sending out dozens of questionnaires, her questionnaire was tested out. On her computer Lucy made several versions, cutting out and simplifying questions where necessary, and wrote various explanations as to how to complete it until she was happy that the questionnaire was likely to be successful. She also ensured that the questionnaire was well presented, not too long, and avoided asking personal and insensitive questions.

Lucy was aware that sending out questionnaires 'cold' through the post is both unethical and might elicit a poor response rate. Hence she wrote, telephoned and emailed the various gatekeepers of institutions she wished to survey to find out if they were interested in completing the questionnaire and obtained consent to send it. She also used her personal contacts in the various professions. Such personal contact prior to sending out the questionnaires ensured a very high response rate for Lucy. Out of 70 questionnaires that were sent out to the various professionals, 59 were returned, which is a response rate of 84 per cent.

Lucy sent an information pack to those organisations that had shown an interest in the study. She sent this pack to some organisations by email and to others through the regular post. Both the email and post pack contained the following:

- A university-headed letter confirming the researcher's identity (see Chapter 3 on ethics). This included Lucy's telephone number and email address if there were any questions.
- A consent form which requested that the professional sign the sheet to show that he/she had read the accompanying letters and informing him/her that the research was anonymous.
- A letter outlining the overall purposes of the study and how the research will hopefully benefit their profession (Figure 9.3). Lucy put the date when she needed the questionnaire to be returned in capital letters.
- The questionnaire itself (Figure 9.4).
- A stamped self-addressed envelope.

The Uptown University College,
Uptown Road,
Uptown.

Email: Lucy@uptownuni.com

Mobile: 07790 – 675423

10 November

Dear Sir/Madam,
Further to the telephone conversation I had with you concerning my research project on Domestic Violence, I am enclosing the Questionnaire. Please see the accompanying letter which confirms my identity and status as a student at Uptown University College studying for the BA/BSc in Early Childhood Studies.

I am writing to you as I would like to invite you to take part in this research. I must stress that you will remain anonymous and that if at any point during the research study you wish to withdraw, you may do so.

The aim of the anonymous study is to gain different professionals' perspectives on whether domestic violence issues should be raised in schools and, indeed, whether it is an appropriate topic to discuss with primary-aged school children.

My timescale for this study is very limited, so I would be grateful if you could complete the attached questionnaire and return it in the enclosed stamped addressed envelope BY THE 30 NOVEMBER.

Thank you very much for taking the time to read this letter. I hope that you are interested in this study and are willing to take part. After I have completed the study I will send you a précis of my findings.

If you have any comments, suggestions or questions please do contact me by email at the above address.

Yours sincerely,
Lucy Holden

Figure 9.3   Letter outlining the purpose of the study

The Uptown University College,
Uptown Road,
Uptown.

Email: Lucy@uptownuni.com

Mobile: 07790 – 675423

Professional's Questionnaire: Domestic Violence

Please state your profession ....

Q1)   In your professional capacity have you had contact with or been approached by a child over concerns of domestic violence?
(Please tick appropriate box)

Yes: ☐   No: ☐

Q2)   Were you able to listen to and support their concerns?
(Please tick appropriate box)

Yes: ☐   No: ☐   Never been approached: ☐

Q2a) If yes to question 2 were you then able to address these concerns?
(Please tick appropriate box)

Yes: ☐   No: ☐   If No, why? ....

Q3)   If yes, to question 2a – To what degree did you feel successful?
(Please tick appropriate box)

Very Successful	Successful	Adequately	Unsuccessful	Very Unsuccessful

Other ....

Q4)   Do you feel it is your place to answer questions on the issue of domestic violence?

If yes, why? ....
If no, why? ....

Q5)   Is there a designated member of your organisation who is responsible for dealing with the issue of domestic violence?
(Please tick appropriate box)

Yes: ☐   No: ☐   Unsure: ☐

If yes, who ....

Q6   If yes to Question 5 – What action can the designated person take?

....
....

Q7)   In some schools recently there have been initiatives (Hackney & Westminster) to address domestic violence through PSHE (citizenship). Do you have any knowledge of similar practices in your area?
(Please tick appropriate box)

Yes: ☐   No: ☐   Don't know: ☐

Q8) Do you think it is appropriate to include the issue of domestic violence within the National Curriculum in primary schools?
(Please tick appropriate box)

Yes: ☐   No: ☐   Unsure: ☐

Q9) When would it be appropriate to introduce the subject of domestic violence into the School Curriculum?
(Please tick appropriate box)

| 4–7 years | 7–9years | 9–11years | Secondary Education | Not Appropriate |

Q10) Do you think domestic violence could be prevented or reduced through education in primary schools?
(Please tick appropriate box)

Yes: ☐   No: ☐   Unsure: ☐

Thank you very much for taking the time to fill out this questionnaire, it is much appreciated, please feel free to attach additional sheets and add any other comments.

Figure 9.4   Questionnaire

Case study

Ruth's study concerned female nursery workers' perceptions of working with male colleagues in two all-female staffed nurseries.

At a staff meeting Ruth explained that she wanted to know more about the attitudes of female staff and possible barriers that men faced in working in nurseries. She asked for the staff's opinions on methods and they suggested surveying the staff with questionnaires and follow-up interviews. Subsequently Ruth wrote and handed out questionnaires with sealable envelopes to all the staff. Due to the sensitive nature of the topic, Ruth decided to place a home-made 'post box' in the staff room, for completed questionnaires to be posted in their envelopes. This post box ensured anonymity because Ruth did not know who the questionnaires were from and, because of the ease of 'posting' in the staffroom, she got a high response rate. Ruth found that the questionnaire stimulated so much interest that nearly all the respondents were happy to discuss further the issues raised by it.

Writing your questionnaire

In order successfully to write your questionnaire you need to be absolutely clear about what it is your research is concerned with and exactly what you wish to find out. There is no space on a questionnaire for ambiguity or vagueness (Denscombe, 2007). A questionnaire that is too long is probably the major reason why people do not complete questionnaires. Two sides of A4 paper should be sufficient for most questionnaires.

The following is a list of points to bear in mind when writing your questionnaire:

- At the top you should write a short explanation/rationale for the questionnaire if this is not already included in a separate covering letter.

- Include a statement concerning the anonymity of the respondent.

- Is the appearance and layout straightforward?

- Is the language simple?

- Have you avoided leading questions? (e.g. 'Do you agree that …?')

- Are the questions short, clear and unambiguous?

- Is there a minimum of technical jargon?

- Do your questions go from easiest to most difficult?

- Have you thanked the respondents at the end?

Different types of questions

Using a questionnaire, carried out with early childhood studies students, Figure 9.5 demonstrates six different types of questions that you can write including:

- making a list

- a closed question Yes/No answer

- agree, disagree with a statement

- choosing from a list of options

- placing reasons in a rank order

- open-ended questions.

Student Motivations for Joining the Early Childhood Studies Degree

I am interested in the diverse reasons for students doing the Early Childhood Studies degree course. Your responses will provide Course Tutors with knowledge about why you are studying for the degree, which will help us to understand your needs better! This is an anonymous questionnaire so please try to answer honestly!

Male   Female   *Please circle*

Age:

[A list]
Please list 3 issues which motivated you to study for the Early Childhood Studies Degree.

1.

2.

3.

[A closed question Yes/No answer]
Was Early Childhood Studies your first choice of degree? *Please tick*

Yes: ☐   No: ☐

If no, what did you wish to study?

[Agree/disagree with a statement (the Likert scale)]
Generally speaking I am happy to be studying for the Early Childhood Studies Degree.
Please circle ONE.

Definitely agree   Agree to some extent   Disagree

[Rank order]
From the following list of reasons as to why you initially chose to do the Early Childhood Studies degree, choose the THREE which you feel are most appropriate to you.

1 = strongest reason   2 = second strongest reason   3 = third strongest reason

Employment opportunities after Graduation are good.
The only course I could get on to.
I want to work with children.
I want to help the country to meet the need for Early Childhood workers.
I'm not sure what I want to do yet, so the course gives me some time to think.
Working with children is an interesting and worthwhile job.

[Open-ended questions]
What work do you wish to do when you leave University with your Early Childhood Studies Degree?
Is there anything else you wish to say concerning your reasons for studying the Early Childhood Studies Degree?

Many thanks indeed for your help.

Figure 9.5

When you write your questionnaire it is a good idea to include a variety, not necessarily all, of these types of questions to keep the respondent interested in the survey. Using a variety of questions also generates different forms of evidence which you can subsequently use.

Writing a Likert scale questionnaire

This is a common form of questionnaire and can be successfully used to measure people's attitudes.

1. *Write down a list of statements* that are significant and important to the respondents in your topic area. These statements can be identified from your reading in the area and informal discussions with the respondents themselves. The statements should be written as both a positive and a negative and there should be approximately the same number of positive and negative statements.

2. *Categorise the responses* by having five fixed-alternative expressions, labelled: agree strongly; agree; unsure; disagree; disagree strongly

3. *Ask a number of respondents* to complete the Likert scale questionnaire.

📁 **Case study**

Using the Likert scale questionnaire

Jane posted out a Likert scale questionnaire to approximately 80 early years professionals (EYPs) in her local authority (Figure 9.6). She wanted to find out more about the extent to which early years professionals were able to lead learning in their settings. Jane knew that the EYPs were very busy practitioners and unlikely to complete a lengthy questionnaire. Hence she compiled the following straightforward and easy to use Likert questionnaire. In addition to the Likert scale, Jane included some questions which helped her to contextualise the EYP. Jane was able to follow up these questionnaires by asking a random sample of the EYPs to further expand why they had ticked particular statements. She was then able to follow up the questionnaire with six of the EYPs in a focus group setting when they met for their monthly Network Meeting.

Early Years Professional Status Research Project

Dear Early Years Professionals,

We would like to know your comments and views about your role as an Early Years Professional (EYP) in your setting. EYPs are considered to be important in raising the quality of early years provision. They are expected to act as 'change agents' to improve practice, and lead practice across the Early Years Foundation Stage. I would like to explore this with you by inviting you to complete the attached questionnaire in which you will be given an opportunity to reflect upon your role as an EYP.

Completing this questionnaire will help us to widen our understanding of EYPs. Your information will be analysed and treated in confidence. You and your setting will NOT be identifiable in the results. We ask for your name and setting information so that we might potentially contact you by telephone or email to ask you further questions.

Please ensure that you return your questionnaire to us by Friday February 12th.

POST: A.N. Other, University of Poppleton.
EMAIL: a.n.other@poppleton.ac.uk

We look forward to reading your views.
With many thanks and best wishes,
A.N.Other

If you wish to ask any further information please email us or call me on 07983 234 567

Name:
Name of setting:
Email address:

Contextual information about you and your setting – please tick or put a cross in the box

1. Type of early years setting in which you work:

Private daycare	
Children's Centre	
Sessional daycare	
Childminder	
Other (describe)	

2. Number of years worked in the early years sector:

0–2 years	
3–5 years	
6–10 years	
11–15 years	
16–20 years	
21–25 years	
26–30 years	

(Continued)

(Continued)

3. Year EYPS gained

2006	
2007	
2008	
2009	
2010 (awaiting moderation)	

4. EYPS Pathway undertaken

Validation	
Long	
Short	
Full	

5. Qualifications on entry to EYPS Pathway

Degree with subject Early Years/Early Childhood	
Foundation Degree in Early Years	
Degree in Education	
Qualified Teacher Status	
Another subject (not early years) degree	
Not a degree qualification	
Masters Degree	
Other	

6. Have you gained new employment since achieving EYPS?

Yes	
No	

With the following statements please indicate your preference with a cross or tick and explain your answers in further detail.

Statement	Strongly Agree	Agree	Not Sure	Disagree	Strongly Disagree
1. My role as an EYP is not important					

Statement	Strongly Agree	Agree	Not Sure	Disagree	Strongly Disagree
2. My role as an EYP is clear to me					

Statement	Strongly Agree	Agree	Not Sure	Disagree	Strongly Disagree
3. My role as an EYP is unclear to my colleagues					

Statement	Strongly Agree	Agree	Not Sure	Disagree	Strongly Disagree
4. I am supported in my role as an EYP in my setting					

Statement	Strongly Agree	Agree	Not Sure	Disagree	Strongly Disagree
5. I am not supported in my role as an EYP in other contexts					

Statement	Strongly Agree	Agree	Not Sure	Disagree	Strongly Disagree
6. I am able to lead learning in my setting					

Statement	Strongly Agree	Agree	Not Sure	Disagree	Strongly Disagree
7. I am not able to implement change in my setting					

Statement	Strongly Agree	Agree	Not Sure	Disagree	Strongly Disagree
8. I am able to reflect upon my leadership practices					

Statement	Strongly Agree	Agree	Not Sure	Disagree	Strongly Disagree
9. My professional development needs are not being met					

10. In this space please feel free to let me know anything else about being an EYP

Thank you very much for completing this questionnaire.

Figure 9.6

Summary ☐

This chapter has:

- developed your understanding of the different uses of questionnaires

- demonstrated the different ways in which to write questionnaires

- reviewed the way in which questionnaires can form part of your triangulation.

Recommended reading 📖

Denscombe, M. (2007) *The Good Research Guide*. Maidenhead: Open University Press.
Chapter 1 of this user-friendly introductory guide to research focuses upon the survey approach whilst Chapter 9 is concerned with writing questionnaires. Both chapters are recommended as together they offer the novice researcher a good foundation in the use of the survey design and the questionnaire method.

Siraj-Blatchford, J. (2010) 'Surveys and questionnaires: An evaluative case study', in G. MacNaughton, S. Rolfe and I. Siraj-Blatchford (eds) *Doing Early Childhood Research: International Perspectives on Theory and Practice*, 2nd edn. Buckingham: Open University Press.
This chapter provides an interesting discussion about the ways in which to use questionnaires combined with interviews in a small-scale survey. The chapter includes a useful overview of the research design and sampling issues needed when carrying out a small-scale survey.

10 Analysing your data

Learning objectives

This chapter will help you to:

- understand that analysing your data involves combining it with literature in your chosen field
- understand that sorting out your data requires you to organise and catalogue your data
- consider the use of Excel and NVivo
- know how to generate categories, themes and headings into which you place your data
- examine some detailed analysis examples.

The chapter in which you analyse your data is often the central part of your research study and for some may be the longest section. This is a crucial chapter since it brings together and combines all the data you have collected with your literature review. You then build and write an argument using both your data and the literature. You have collected a lot of data during your research project and now you have to make sense of all that wonderful data both for yourself and the readers of your project. A commonly used way to make sense of your data is to reduce it and then to display it. Reducing your data means that you should try to generate key themes, concepts or 'headlines' from your data. Compiling themes needs careful organisation and may be represented in the following process.

The process of organising your data

1. What does the literature say about the issues you are researching (see Chapter 5)? How can you use these ideas to help organise your data?

2. How does your data agree with, build upon and contradict the literature in your topic area?

3. Now look at the data you have collected. What is it that your data is telling you?

4. How does your data answer your initial research questions?

5. What themes, categories or headings do you think emerge from your data (see Figure 10.1)? You can code your different topics or pieces of data as shown in the example later in this chapter.

6. Do not organise your data according to research techniques or as to whether it is qualitative or quantitative data but, rather, integrate all your different sources of data together and place under content themes.

7. How are these themes related to the literature in the area? These thematic categories or headings may arise from the literature as well as be your own creations.

8. Do the themes you have chosen connect and link together?

9. What is it you want to say? What are the main arguments running through the whole discussion of your data?

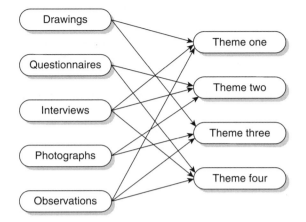

Figure 10.1   How different pieces of data are placed into different themes

10. Organising your data involves a process known as topic coding. Topic coding simply involves labelling your data and sorting it out into different topics. Coding can be done in a variety of ways. An example is given later in this chapter. Topic coding can be done using the computer to highlight pieces of similar data using different colours for each theme. You might also wish to cut and paste the interview data and key pieces of questionnaires and drawings into differently named computer files using the topic theme headings. This can also be done in Word or the more specialised programme known as NVivo. (Be sure to keep all this data safe by backing it up onto a pen drive and/or emailing it to yourself).

11. Sometimes pieces of data do not fall neatly into one theme or another but, rather, can be placed into two or more themes. That is fine, the data can be used under both themes!

12. If you have large amounts of data under each topic you need to select the best and richest pieces. What makes these pieces so interesting? Why have you selected these and not others? How do the pieces you have selected add to your developing argument?

13. Under each thematic or topic heading discuss the pieces of data you have selected with what the literature says about the issues. This produces your discussion, as in Figure 10.2.

Figure 10.2 How themes discussed with literature produce a discussion (adapted from Holliday, 2002: 113)

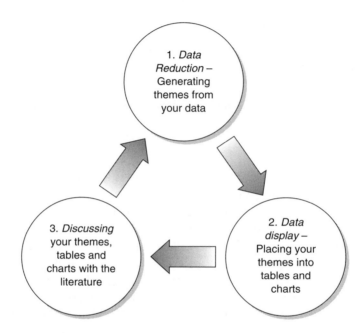

Figure 10.3 Figure showing relationship between data reduction, display and discussion

Reducing and displaying your data

Generating your themes from your data is the first part of data reduction. You are reducing the mass of observations and interviews into a few core key themes or 'headlines'. The second part of data reduction is to display those key themes or core ideas in tables and charts. Figure 10.3 outlines this process of data reduction and display.

The themes that you have compiled can be displayed in tables. This process of reducing and displaying your data will further help you to understand the data and this makes analysis easier. As Miles and Huberman (1994: 11) succinctly state 'You know what you display'. Organising and sorting your themes into tables certainly helps to clarify the issues that arise from the data.

In the following example an early years student is researching the extent to which different nurseries engage with the Early Years Foundation Stage requirement (DCSF, 2008) that children must play outdoors for at least part of each day. The student has purposively sampled two nurseries that she knows have different ways of outdoor working with the children. She has used questionnaires, interviews and observations to collect her data. She has gone through the steps outlined above and has compiled eight main themes from her questionnaires, interviews and observations. These main themes are presented below. The display helps to draw out similarities and differences between each nursery.

Key Outdoor Play Themes in the Two Nurseries

Themes	Low Field Nursery	Spring Garden Nursery
1. Space	Lack of space – hard concrete area; overgrown bushes; mud	Large garden and field – range of grass, trees and bushes
2. Practitioners' training	Practitioners apprehensive about health and safety issues	Practitioners all attended outdoor spaces workshop and feel confident outdoors
3. Clothing	Many children come in poor quality outdoor clothes	Parents are aware of providing children with good quality outdoors clothing
4. Gender issues	Girls reluctant to participate outdoors	Boys and and girls enjoying outdoors
5. Staff ratios	Insufficient staff hence outdoor ratios problematic	Sufficient staff to cover outdoor ratios
6. Resources	Few wheelies; dirty sandpit; broken furniture	Bikes, scooters, swings, slides, sandpit, large hill, climbing apparatus, outdoor water area
7. Context	Busy road next to nursery	Quiet area

Using Excel and NVivo software for analysis

Computer software such as Excel and NVivo is an excellent way to help you organise, analyse and display your data. But it must be remembered that any software package is a tool for analysis – it cannot do it for you. In the above outdoor research project the student made a questionnaire using the Likert scale and distributed it to 20 practitioners. She distributed the same questionnaire to an equal number of practitioners in both Low Field Nursery and Spring Garden Nursery. Figures 10.4 and 10.5 show a compilation of the number of responses from the 20 questionnaires from each of the nurseries.

To what extent is the outdoor space utilised in Low Field Nursery?					
	Strongly Agree	Agree	Unsure	Disagree	Strongly Disagree
I am happy to work with the children outdoors	11		7	2	
I like the outdoor requirement in the EYFS	5	3	12		
We have enough staff to cover the ratios outdoors			10	5	5
I have not attended outdoor training courses	17			3	
The children come with adequate clothing		4	7		9
The parents are unhappy when the children get wet	15	3		2	
Both boys and girls spend same amount of time outdoors		3	12	5	
There are insufficient resources for the outdoors	14	3	3		
I want to spend more time outdoors	2	6	1	3	6
Children need to be outdoors for long periods	4		10	6	

Figure 10.4 Excel table of Low Field Nursery questionnaire responses from 20 completed questionnaires

Within the Excel programme the questionnaire data above can be transformed into graphs and the two data sets can then be compared. Such graphical representation of the data helps with the analysis of the findings. It certainly demonstrates how different nurseries are in their interpretation of the Early Years Foundation Stage outdoor requirements.

NVivo (formerly known as NUDIST) is a complex and sophisticated computer software package that your college or university may have on their computers. It is increasingly used in the analysis of qualitative data since it is so potentially powerfully. It is a flexible program that enables the researcher to store a wide range of digital data including photos, videos, drawings, interviews and questionnaire data. Within NVivo all the data is given labels or codes and connections are then built up between the codes in a tree structure.

To what extent is the outdoor space utilised in Spring Garden Nursery?	Strongly Agree	Agree	Unsure	Disagree	Strongly Disagree
I am happy to work with the children outdoors	17		3		
I like the outdoor requirement in the EYFS	12	8			
We have enough staff to cover the ratios outdoors	10	5	5		
I have not attended outdoor training courses		1		3	16
The children come with adequate clothing	9	4	7		
The parents are unhappy when the children get wet		1	3	2	14
Both boys and girls spend same amount of time outdoors	11	3	4	2	
There are insufficient resources for the outdoors			3	6	11
I want to spend more time outdoors	10	6	4		
Children need to be outdoors for long periods	14	3	2	1	

Figure 10.5   Excel table of Spring Garden Nursery questionnaire responses from 20 completed questionnaires

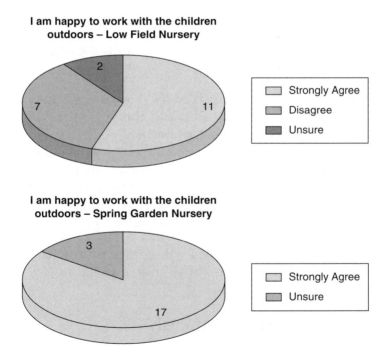

Figure 10.6   Graphs generated in Excel from data in Figures 10.4 and 10.5

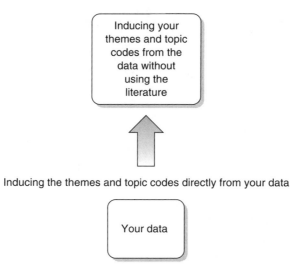

Figure 10.7   Diagram showing the themes being induced from the data

Inducing and/or deducing the themes and topic codes

When generating your themes or topic codes it is possible to go directly up from the data as in Figure 10.7.

In Figure 10.7 you have no pre-specified codes that you impose upon your data. You simply let the data suggest the codes and themes. At the other end of the spectrum you might be working with pre-specified codes that you have already decided are important and you impose these upon the data and put the data into these pre-established themes or topics. These topics might come directly from the literature or a similar research project to yours. Here you simply wish to import topic codes or themes into your project. This is known as deducing the themes or topic areas from the literature (see Figure 10.8).

In reality your themes and topic codes will come from both your own ideas about the data and from the literature in your area as Figure 10.9 demonstrates.

Topic coding in qualitative analysis

Even if you are not using NVivo, your qualitative data analysis will involve topic coding. Coding is simply a process of classifying chunks of your interview data and

Deducing the themes and codes from the literature in your area

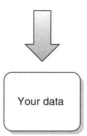

Figure 10.8   Diagram showing the themes being deduced from the literature onto your data

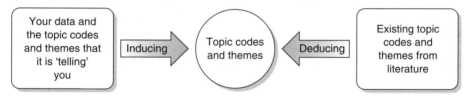

Figure 10.9   Diagram showing topic themes coming from both your data and the literature

observations into key themes or headlines. Coding involves placing labels or tags onto those chunks of qualitative data. These chunks of data can then be placed together under themes or headlines. In the following example from the outdoors project discussed above chunks of data have been coded as follows from the following short interview transcript with a practitioner from Spring Garden Nursery.

'I think the fact that the EYFS says that you have to take the children out everyday is really good news. We've always done that but now that the curriculum states we should do it is supportive and encouraging of what I believe in really' (1).

(Continued)

(Continued)

'At this nursery I have to say that we really like playing and working with the children in the outdoors here. I think this is partly because some of us went on a training course (2) and I have had a lot of outdoor type experience myself when I was growing up. I feel really confident taking the children out and giving them outdoor experiences. We have a small back yard space (3) and covered area where we have sand and water play and a few wheelies. The boys in particular seem to benefit from being outdoors – they are always out there. We have to monitor that and see that the girls use it just as much.' (4)

'Although we don't have a big garden ourselves there's a fantastic bit of woodland just round the corner from here (5). It's about 10 minutes walk away. The older children love going in there as it's like a natural wilderness. We have had campfires in there and sung songs around the fire. In the summer we have picnics in there together and the children love it and so do I! (5) We even go out there in the rain sometimes. We have a saying that there is no such thing as bad weather only bad clothing! (6). Some of the parents don't like it though 'cos the children get a bit muddy and especially if they don't have boots and so on – that's really frustrating. We still have to educate them to realise that mud is not dangerous (7). Sometimes we don't have enough staff to take the children out because we have to keep to the children/staff ratios (8)'.

Some possible topic codes or headlines emerging the interview above:

1. EYFS stipulation supporting practitioners' existing beliefs
2. Training giving confidence
3. Limited space and resources for outdoor play
4. Gender and outdoor space
5. Being imaginative with nearby outdoor spaces
6. Lack of appropriate clothes for some children
7. Parental concerns
8. Insufficient staff.

Using these eight broad topic codes or themes it is now possible to go through all the other transcripts and identify those pieces of interview data and observations that might fit under these topic codes or headlines. In this way it is possible to collate the data together under the above topic codes. The data is then interrogated with the literature to produce a more detailed and thorough analysis.

Coding in this manner is how NVivo works too. If you have the time to use NVivo you will find that it is a powerful tool that enables you to make creative and imaginative connections and linkages across your different data sets. Despite the undoubted uses of computer software, however, there is no substitute for a close reading and scrutiny of your data alongside the published literature.

Analysing your data

When you sit down after you have collected all your data and begin to reflect upon what you have got, you might be surprised at the volume of data you have accumulated. Some small-scale research reports include a vast amount of data in the text and in the appendices, whilst other reports have less. What is important is not the volume of the data but, rather, the quality of the data and what you do with it in the discussion section of your report. Try to incorporate as many different forms of data as you can to help provide triangulation and thus increase the validity of your arguments.

Hopefully you will have a range of different forms of data, for example:

observations

interviews with children and adults

drawings children have made

questionnaire data

photographs children have taken

your research diary.

Knowing the literature in your topic area will greatly assist you with the process of identifying the significant data you have collected. Being well versed in the literature is essential, since you will be able immediately to spot issues arising from your data that are also discussed in the literature. First-time early childhood researchers are often unsure about what data to incorporate in their discussion and what to leave out. This process of matching up and discussing, 'interrogating' and breaking down what you found in the interviews, questionnaires and drawings, with what the literature says, is at the heart of a good discussion and analysis section. Hence, a good knowledge of the literature in your topic area is critical in helping you successfully to analyse your data.

The fragments of data which are chosen will be 'rich' in the sense of containing key aspects of your developing argument (Holliday, 2007). You must *tell* the reader what you believe the data extract to be saying – what do you feel the data you have selected contributes to your arguments? The key to your discussion is to tell a story of why you are using the data that you do use. Data cannot simply be left as it is –you must organise it. The data is broken up and selected pieces are used under different thematic headings.

The selection of the data that you use and do not use can be difficult, especially when you decide not to use some of the data you have so painstakingly collected. However, there is little point in including material which, upon reflection, you judge does not further your arguments and may seem irrelevant to your discussion.

There are several questions to ask yourself as you organise and sort out your data:

1. What is the point of this data?

2. Why have I selected it?

3. What is it telling me?

4. How does the data I have chosen further the arguments?

It is important to state why you have chosen a particular piece of data. Choosing data is often to do with the construction of an argument or idea which you believe in and wish your study to highlight. In the following interview on Sarah's gender and friendship research study, she describes the main argument that she wishes to discuss in her analysis section.

> I guess that my main argument throughout the analysis section was to do with the old nature/nurture argument. The nature argument states that girls play with girls and boys play with boys because they are genetically different and hence it is in their nature to do so. The nurture argument on the other hand states that boys are socialised in one way and girls are socialised in another so that's why they are different. The data that I have collected points to both sides of the argument. Both the nature and the nurture arguments can be supported by the small amount of data that I have collected ... My work only scrapes the surface of the issues – I mean there's so much more I need to look at ... but if pushed I think that the nurture argument is more persuasive. I believe this because I have so much data that shows the diversity and complexity of being a boy and a girl. Girls weren't born wearing pink dresses, it's more than just genes!

I suppose what I have tried to do with the data is to select those pieces which highlight the diversity of children's experiences because it's all too easy to confirm the stereotypes. What's the point in that? Stereotypes don't lead us anywhere. It's the data which adds to the complexity of children's gendered behaviour that particularly interests me. I guess this interest comes from reading so much of the nature/socialisation literature but then it was just so interesting!

Notice how Sarah's arguments slowly began to take shape and *emerged* from the data that she had collected. From carrying out a thorough literature review Sarah knew what the main arguments in the area were. But she remained open to what her data suggested to her. As she examined and reflected upon the data in front of her, she realised that the children's pictures and interviews were telling her of the complexity of their friendships. Hence the story or arguments that arose in the analysis section came about from Sarah's reading and her data combined.

Use a wide range of data

It is also important that your research tells the complexity of a story. Try to avoid using your data to make black and white arguments – early childhood issues are usually not polarised in such a simple way. Often people and institutions act in contradictory and sometimes incoherent ways. Practitioners and parents might say one thing about their practice with children but, when you observe them, do another. If possible your research data should discuss such contradictions. Such contradictions will show the readers that your research has captured the complexities of the research respondents and their institutions. What pressures and factors lead people to such contradictory behaviour?

If you can include a range of 'voices' offering alternative perspectives in your discussion, this will inevitably lead to such complexity. The Mosaic approach, discussed in Chapter 7, encourages the 'voices' of children, adults and practitioners. Such a range of 'voices' encourages different perspectives on the same issue to emerge. Such a range of perspectives and ideas from different people makes the research more convincing. People experience early childhood institutions in different ways and hence the research would be unconvincing if all the different groups thought exactly the same way about the research issue. Different ways of seeing the same thing and, sometimes, disagreements can be healthy for an institution's development. Your research report should reflect any such differences.

Generating categories and themes

Just as it is best not to organise your analysis under different research methods, so it also best not to separate out your data according to whether it is qualitative or quantitative. Integrate all your research techniques and their findings together under the different content themes. Work with both the qualitative and quantitative data together. Whilst qualitative data in the form of pictures and interviews and observations takes up a lot space and accounts for many words, the opposite is true of quantitative data. You may have collected a large number of questionnaires but, once you have compiled the statistical information into a handful of graphs and charts, your pile of data will have shrunk considerably.

Knowing the literature in your field will help you to recognise the different themes which emerge from your data. Themes have often been growing in the researcher's mind throughout the whole research process. Themes provide headings for discussion and stages in the argument. Key themes in your research topic might be reflected in some of the data your project has generated. Such themes and categories form the basis and structure of your data analysis. The case study which follows shows how Sarah generated themes from the data she had collected.

Notice how Sarah did not organise her analysis under the different research techniques that she used such as 'drawing data', 'interview data' and 'observational data'. Rather, she combined the data from the drawings, interviews and observations under the different thematic headings. It is the themes that drive the presentation and organisation of the data rather than the different research techniques. This combination of different research techniques adds to the validity of her findings and thus the arguments.

Activity

As you read Sarah's analysis in the case study below, answer the following questions:

- How are the three themes linked together?
- What are Sarah's arguments?
- How does Sarah build her arguments from the data and the literature?
- How does Sarah integrate her data with the literature?

- What forms of evidence has Sarah used?
- Are you convinced by Sarah's analysis and arguments?
- Are you provided with sufficient data to make your own judgements and interpretations?
- Has Sarah explained why she has chosen the data presented?

Case study

How I sorted my material into categories

Sarah told me the following about how she had organised and made sense of all the data she had collected for her project:

I was really pleased that my data supported the literature in that although in the early years of schooling children do *tend* to choose same gender friendships in the classroom and playground, there are also many children who will play happily with both genders. I had seen boys playing with girls and enjoying their company and some girls playing with boys – I wanted to include this. Such selection of data was important because it told a complex story of children's friendships.

I organised material in an old-fashioned way! I sat on the floor and I looked through all the children's pictures of their friends, the observations I had made, and the interview transcripts. I couldn't believe the amount of data from the teachers and the children that I had collected using the taped interviews. It was great that I had so much material but at first it was a bit daunting.

The data was definitely telling me about the complexity of children's relationships – their friendships were largely gendered but there was also some data which seemed to point in a different direction. After a while reading and re-reading the interview data and looking at the pictures I began to see that there were three distinct themes emerging: friendship groups; indoor/outdoor differences in friendship groups; gendered friendship qualities.

I first looked for interesting 'juicy quotes' – these are things that people said to me and things I saw about which I had an immediate gut feeling that they were significant for the project. They're the sort of things that people tell you and you just know immediately that they really stand out. Knowing the literature in the area really helped me to do this! I used three different coloured pens and marked these 'juicy quotes' in red for friendships between girls, black for friendships between the boys and blue for friendships between the girls and the boys. There were about 10 juicy quotes in all. Then I looked more closely and saw that some of the children's quotes confirmed the stereotypes about boys playing with boys and girls playing with girls whilst other quotes contradicted this. These juicy quotes seemed to fit into three fairly distinct themes. I actually used scissors to cut out these juicy bits and put them into the three piles on the floor. I then selected the most interesting pictures.

The following is a case study of Sarah's analysis. It is included at some length to show the way in which data and literature are intertwined under the three thematic headings. Before this section Sarah had written about her research techniques and why she had chosen to use them.

Case study

Sarah's research on gender in a Year 1 classroom – discussion of findings

Friendship groups

The drawing, observational and interview data that I collected pointed towards a tendency for same-sex friendships. However, the data from these different sources could also be interpreted as showing that some children had mixed-gender friendship groups. Small groups of children, 22 in all, were asked to draw a picture of themselves playing with their friends. Each drawing was analysed by asking the following questions:

- What was the sex of the drawer?
- What was the sex of the children drawn?
- What games did the drawing show?

The drawings produced some interesting quantitative and qualitative data. Sixty per cent of the girls and 80 per cent of the boys drew children of their sex only. This finding may be graphically represented in the pie charts in Figures 10.10 and 10.11.

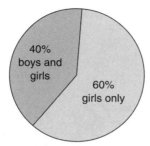

Figure 10.10   Sixty per cent of girls drew only other girls as their friends

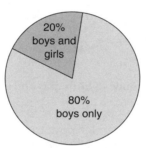

Figure 10.11   Eighty per cent of boys drew only other boys as their friends

The data from the pie charts may be interpreted to suggest that there is clear evidence of single-sex bias in the friendships of the Year 1 class. No claim is made for the statistical reliability of the findings since there were only 22 drawings made in the one classroom. This finding echoes previous research, which has noted sex-based friendships as a characteristic of children's peer relationships (Erwin, 1998; Jacklin and Lacey, 1997; Maccoby, 1996). The development of this same-sex friendship preference has been considered to run parallel to the development of gender identity itself (Erwin, 1998). At first sight the drawing data would appear to confirm that children's understandings of what it means to be a boy or girl within the cultural and social contexts of their worlds, leads them to establish and maintain relationships largely with same-sex peers.

However, the fact that 40 per cent of the girls drew girls *and* boys as being their friends and that 20 per cent of the boys included girls as their friends needs discussing (Figure 10.12). That twice as many girls drew boys as their friends than boys drew girls as their friends suggests that it may be more acceptable

I play football with _____ when he asks because he is always kind to me.

Figure 10.12   Chantel's picture showing both girls and boys as her friends

for girls to play with boys than for boys to play with girls. That this interpretation may be made from this small-scale study is confirmed by Epstein (1998: 107) who has noted that 'for a girl, being more boyish means being more powerful in the world. For a boy to be more female is to be less powerful'. That 40 per cent of the girls chose boys amongst their friends but only 20 per cent of the boys chose girls as their friends confirms this assertion. This finding is also given support by Skelton (2001: 78) who has claimed that it is rarer to see boys 'crossing over' the gender divide to play with girls than for girls to cross over and play with boys. Indeed, one of the girls interviewed was proud of playing mainly with boys: 'My Mum says I play with boys 'cos I'm a Tomboy you see.'

Although Colin drew mainly girls in his picture and according to my observations often played with girls, he denied that he did so in a subsequent group interview. Colin's contradictory behaviour may perhaps be explained by Epstein's (1998) argument above that boys lose power within a patriarchal society by regularly playing with girls. Skelton (2001) has noted that within a school context, boys who engage with feminine stereotypical play may make themselves vulnerable to teasing by other boys and girls. Thus for boys to play with girls may be potentially problematic in that bullying of the boy may occur. Mac An Ghail (1994) has noted that 'schools operate as masculine making devices' and Epstein (1998: 12) has noted that schools are 'particularly difficult places for boys to depart from the norm'. That Colin denied that he played with girls may be because boys and girls actively 'police' each other's genders thereby reinforcing stereotypical gendered behaviour (MacNaughton, 2000). Perhaps in the context of a group interview with other boys present Colin would make himself too vulnerable if he said he mostly played with girls. Upon reflection, a group interview with Colin and some girls may have been a more appropriate context in which to interview Colin.

A content analysis of the children's play by sex confirms Craft's (1994) argument that children tend to hold stereotypical views about what it is appropriate for boys to play and what it is appropriate for girls to play. The boys overwhelmingly chose aggressive and competitive subjects to draw, such as dinosaurs, football and action men, whilst the girls chose to draw more gentle and home-based activities such as Barbie dolls and painting. My observations of the children in the playground confirmed that some boys were engaged in more physical activities than some girls. Such shared similar play interests serve to develop the relationships between the girls and between the boys respectively. They develop their separate interests and skills together, building upon their expertise in these different activities.

The above arguments concerning the ways in which children 'police' each other's behaviour (Epstein, 1998; Mac An Ghail, 1994; Skelton, 2001) may have influenced the children's drawings. That the drawings were carried out by the children sitting together may have encouraged their stereotypical content. Upon reflection, perhaps the drawings should have been carried out individually but ethically this may not have been appropriate.

My observations of the children both in the classroom and the playground, however, both confirm and contradict the above discussion. My observations showed that whilst some classroom behaviour confirmed some boys as demanding more of the teacher's time than the girls, other boys were quiet, shy and compliant in class. Girls and boys intermingled, chatted and shared work in the classroom.

> (23.1.04 Literacy Hour Group Work; 9.45–10.45.)
> Anne, Jane, Jake, Stuart and Billy are making a shared book together based on 'Brown Bear Brown Bear'. There is much discussion between the children about the organisation and layout of their pictures and writing for their book. Jake and Jane are often seen to be laughing about humorous ideas for their book. They are enjoying each other's company.

This observation shows the way in which children within the classroom context may be socialised to work and play together (MacNaughton, 2000). However, in the different context of the playground the division between boys' and girls' friendship groups was more apparent.

Indoor/outdoor differences in friendship groups

The following observation serves to illustrate some boys physically taking up space and knocking other boys, and girls in particular, out of the way.

> Jake, Ben and Danny are running around the playground, holding hands in a line. The boys are laughing and shouting about what good friends they are. They run around the playground with the line being broken and re-made as they crash into other children. Ben stops to have a drink from the water fountain. Danny pushes him out of the way in a friendly way and tries to get in front of Ben to have a drink himself. Ben pushes him back. 'Hey, what are you doing man?!!!' Ben shouts laughing at the same time. Ben and Danny continue to push each other until the playground teacher tells them to stop and to use all their 'boisterous energy to play a game of football on the grass'. *(28.1.04 Afternoon Playtime 2.30–2.40 pm.)*

The above example shows three boys engaging in an aggressive and dominating physical activity and confirming stereotypical, gendered boys' behaviour. This finding confirms MacNaughton's (2000) view that boys are socialised to take up more playground space and dominate public spaces. The children's behaviour with their friends reflects the societal meanings that they have come to attach to the separate labels of boy and girl. Additionally the teacher and thus the institution confirms the boys' gender and physical dominance by telling them to play football with their high energy levels. This finding confirms Craft's (1994) and MacNaughton's (2000) argument that the schooling process is central in confirming children's gender. But even here there was some mixing. Mostly boys and a handful of girls would play football, taking up a great deal of the playground space, whilst some boys and predominately girls played quietly round the edges with clapping games, talking, imaginative games and games of 'it'. For example, Mary and Charlie enjoyed playing spiderman together in the playground.

Charlie: We have this cool spiderman game where Mary puts her pullover over her shoulders and says 'spiderman' and then I chase her all over the place.

Mary: Yeah, he catches me sometimes then we swop round and he's spiderman.

My observations showed that Charlie and Mary clearly enjoyed each other's company, both in the playground and in the classroom, thus questioning some of the findings which suggest the dominance of single-sex friendship groups. I interviewed the playground assistants and they confirmed my observations.

Gendered friendship qualities

The consultations I had with children about what constitutes a good friend built upon the literature in the area. Maccoby (1996) argues for the existence of gendered friendship qualities, and the data I collected in the drawings, observations and discussions concurs with this. Maccoby suggests that some boys will look for friendships associated with power and excitement. The predominance of football in the boys' drawings and other physical sports supports this view. However, Jake's comment below shows that, whilst boys are aware that being hard physical players and friends is generally a positive friendship attribute, they are aware that aggressive physical force outside a game situation is to be avoided, as demonstrated at the end of the following interview with Jake, Lewis and Jane.

Researcher:	What do you think makes a good friend?
Jake:	I like a friend that is kind to me and helps me with my work and I like a friend that plays football with me. All the boys play football, John, Lewis …
Lewis:	Yeah, yeah, I like a friend that plays football with me and plays with me in the playground.
Jane:	I like a friend that plays with me. I like it when my friends come to my house for a party.
Lewis:	Yeah, I like a friend that comes by my house and plays with my remote controlled car.
Researcher:	So what do you think does not make a good friend?
Jane:	I don't like a friend who puts me down or is mean to me. I don't like a friend that bosses me about.
Jake:	I don't like a friend that hits me. You have to tell before they run to the teacher and tell a lie! Tell that you hit them!!! I don't like people who do that.
Lewis:	Billy isn't my friend when he loses at a game. He always loses and hits other people and then … and then hits me too. He shouldn't do that after we've finished football should he?

Here activity, power and aggression are not characteristics that Jake or Lewis consider to be agreeable in a friend. The language they use mirrors the 'active, invasive, aggressive and bullying' descriptions of bad friends that the boys gave in Craft's (1994: 189) study. Therefore it could be argued, that for some of the boys at least, stereotypical boys' behaviour is not regarded as a positive friendship attribute. Maccoby (1996) contends that girls look for their communal needs to be met through friendship and Jane certainly confirms this in the above interview. However, Jake above also mentions that he likes friends that are kind to him and help him with this work.

Figure 10.13 William and George playing football together

Maccoby believes girls view intimacy, love and communion as positive friendship attributes (Maccoby, 1996). Jane above confirms Maccoby's desired female friendship qualities. However, these were not qualities that were solely confined to the girls' friendship expectations. Concerning his picture (Figure 10.13), William said that George was his friend because George 'helps me', and 'is kind to me' and 'speaks nicely to me'.

The complexity of children's friendships was supported by the classroom teacher's response as to whether she believed the boys and girls in her class looked for different qualities in their friends: 'No ... no. I wouldn't say that. I think boys and girls look for the same things from friendship. They want somebody to play with, be nice to them and play good games ... '.

Jacklin and Lacey (1997) suggest that the impact that the teacher has upon the classroom relationships is important and may well set the tone for friendships within the classroom. They highlight the importance of teacher and school intervention to assure equality and gender integration in early years settings.

Sarah's conclusion

The research question which has guided this study asked what the relationship between gender and friendship was amongst young children. This study has begun to answer this complex relationship. My research study has highlighted a tendency for same-sex friendships. My findings confirm MacNaughton's (2000) work which points towards how societal notions of gender-appropriate behaviour influence children's friendship groups. My research corroborates existing knowledge about peer relations, particularly concerning the qualities that young boys and girls associate with the notion of friendship. My study confirms the literature that suggests friendship is a vehicle that children use to explore their place in the world and that their assumptions about the behaviour of boys and girls is reflected in the friendships they form.

However, my limited timescale and the fact that the study was carried out in just one class of 22 children does not allow me to make any sweeping gen-eralisations. My study merely provides some interesting data about the friendships of the children in a particular class in a rural location and cannot be generalised to the experiences of all six- and seven-year-olds. To improve the study I would have liked to spend more time developing my relationships with the children, which would have provided further insights into their friendships. A comparison of the findings from this class with another group of children in a different location would increase the validity of the results. Any further study needs to include other complicated social variables such as race, class, religion and geographical location upon the peer friendship dynamics. Specifically, 'how are gendered friendships intertwined with race and class?' (Connolly, 1998). I would also like to involve the children's par-ents because so much of how we learn to relate with others is sign-posted by our parents. My study concentrated on between-group differences, namely the differences between boys and girls, rather than in-group differ-ences, namely the differences between all boy or all girl friendships. Such a focus upon one of the genders might allow for a more in-depth analysis rather than attempting to examine the friendship qualities of both genders.

My flaws as a first-time researcher should be acknowledged. I did not want to present myself as an authority figure over the children, yet I did feel my position as an 'objective' researcher was compromised on several occa-sions. I reprimanded the children to a certain extent if they shouted over someone else during the interviews. I wanted my status as an adult to influ-ence the research as little as possible but feel it undoubtedly has. My adult status, perhaps perceived as a student teacher by some, might have caused the children to behave and respond to me and my questions in a particular manner (Alderson, 1995). As an adult perceived to have authority in the school, the children may have tried to provide the answers they thought I wanted to hear. The children's answers may have thus been influenced by the dynamics between the children and myself and the context of the research being carried out in a school situation with all its connotations of expected gendered behaviour and performance (Epstein, 1998).

Sharing your research

Congratulations on successfully completing your research project. Your hard work and determination in getting to this point have furthered your knowledge about yourself and the topic area in which you have been so passionately interested. Your research interest will continue into your present and future work with young children. Your confidence in yourself and your interest area will carry forward into exciting future research and work possibilities.

If you are a student, you might find that your course gives you the chance to share your project with your colleagues. This is good practice to do throughout the course and the process of the research itself. Your fellow students can often make excellent suggestions and recommendations for your research. Making your research public within your college at seminars is a worthwhile endeavour for the development of the research and future research questions. If you have carried out your research within an early childhood institution, you can suggest that you feed back your findings at a staff meeting. You may also provide a summary sheet of your research's conclusions. Before making such a presentation, talk through what you will say and write, with your supervisor, to ensure that whatever you say is ethically sensitive and insightful. The professionals who work in the institution know the constraints and limitations under which they work better than you. You need to think carefully about how your research can build upon current practice in the institution.

Early childhood research is a rapidly expanding field and, hence, there are many outlets for your research project. Email the editors of your professional early years magazines and early years research journals providing them with a succinct overview of your research. Such magazines and journals are often looking for copy and this may well provide an exciting publishing outlet for your research.

Summary

By reading and doing the activities in this chapter you will have:

- understood the process of analysing your data
- evaluated the use of computer analysis

- been made aware of the various ways in which to organise your data
- seen how to integrate your data with the literature
- understood the limited and cautious claims that you can make from your small-scale research project
- understood the importance of reflecting upon how to improve your study in the conclusion

Recommended reading 📖

Richards, L. (2009) *Handling Qualitative Data: A Practical Guide*. London: Sage Publications.
This book provides a very user friendly overview of the whole process of analysing your data. The book is packed full of diagrams and case studies which clearly explain the ways in which researchers analyse their data.

MacNaughton, G. and Hughes, P. (2008) *Doing Action Research in Early Childhood Studies*. Buckingham: Open University Press.
'Step 12: Analyse your data' goes through the whole data process from start to finish. Clear steps are shown in how to code and present your data as well as how to sift through your data for patterns.

References

Alderson, P. (1995) *Listening to children: Ethics and Social Research*. Barkingside: Barnardo's.

Alderson, P. (2004) 'Ethics', in S. Fraser, V. Lewis, S. Ding, M. Kellett and C. Robinson (eds) *Doing Research with Children and Young People*. London: Sage Publications with the Open University.

Alderson, P. (2008) *Young Children's Rights: Exploring Beliefs, Principles and Practice*, 2nd edn. London: Jessica Kingsley.

Atweh, B., Kermis, S. and Weeks, P. (1998) *Action Research in Practice: Partnership for Social Justice in Education*. London: Sage Publications.

Aubery, C., David, T., Godfrey, R. and Thompson, L. (2000) *Early Childhood Educational Research*. London: Routledge.

Barker, M. and Petley, J. (eds) (2001) *Ill Effects: The Media/Violence Debate*. London: Routledge.

Blaxter, L., Hughes, C. and Tight, M. (2010) *How to Research*, 3rd edn. Buckingham: Open University Press.

Booth, T. and Ainscow, M. (2004) *Index for Inclusion: Developing Learning, Participation and Play in Early Years and Childcare*. Bristol: Centre for Studies on Inclusive Education.

Bradshaw, J. (2001) *Poverty: The Outcomes for Children*. London: Family Policy Studies Centre.

Bronfenbrenner, U. (1979) *The Ecology of Human Development: Experiments by Nature and Design*. London: Harvard University Press.

Brooker, L. (2001) 'Interviewing children', in G. MacNaughton, S. Rolfe and I. Siraj-Blatchford (eds) *Doing Early Childhood Research: International Perspectives on Theory and Practice*. Buckingham: Open University Press.

Browne, B. (1998) *Unlearning Discrimination in the Early Years*. Stoke-on-Trent: Trentham Books.

Buckingham, D. (1993) *Children Talking Television: The Making of Television Literacy*. London: Falmer.

Cameron, C., Moss. P. and Owen, C. (1999) *Men in the Nursery: Gender and Caring Work*. London: Paul Chapman Publishing.

Campbell, A., Freedman, E., Boulter, C. and Kirkwood, M. (2003) *Issues and Principles in Educational Research for Teachers*. Nottingham: British Educational Research Association.

Campbell, A., McNamara, O. and Gilroy, P. (2004) *Practitioner and Professional Development in Education*. London: Paul Chapman Publishing.

Children's Workforce Development Council (CWDC) (2010) *On the Right Track: Guidance to the Standards for the Award of Early Years Professional Status*. Available from: http://www.cwdcouncil.org.uk/assets/0000/9008/Guidance_To_Standards. pdf (accessed June 2010).

Christensen, P. and James, A. (2008) *Research with Children: Perspectives and Practices*. London: Falmer Press.

Clark, A. (2005) Beyond listening: *Children's Perspectives on Early Childhood Services*. London: Policy Press.

Clark, A. (2008) *Listening as a Way of Life: Why and How we Listen to Young Children*. London: National Children's Bureau.

Clark, A. and Moss, P. (2005) *Spaces to Play: More Listening to Young Children Using the Mosaic Approach*. London: National Children's Bureau.

Clark, A., McQuail, S. and Moss, P. (2003) *Exploring the Field of Listening to and Consulting with Young Children: Research Report RR445*. London: Department of Education and Skills.

Clarke, P. and Siraj-Blatchford, I. (2000) *Supporting Identity, Diversity and Language in the Early Years*. Buckingham: Open University Press.

Claxon, G. and Carr, M. (2004) 'A Framework for Teaching Learning: the dynamics of disposition', *Early Years*, 24(1).

Clough, P. and Nutbrown, C. (2007) *A Student's Guide to Methodology*, 2nd edn. London: Sage Publications.

Coady, M. (2010) 'Ethics in early childhood research', in G. MacNaughton, S. Rolfe and I. Siraj-Blatchford (eds) *Doing Early Childhood Research: International Perspectives on Theory and Practice*, 2nd edn. Buckingham: Open University Press.

Coates, E. (2002) '"I forgot the sky!" Children's stories contained within their drawings', *International Journal of Early Years Education*, 10(1): 21–35.

Cohen, L., Manion, L. and Morrison, K. (2000) *Research Methods in Education*, 5th edn. London: Routledge.

Connolly, P. (1998) *Racism, Gender Identities and Young Children: Social Relations in a Multi-Ethnic, Inner-City Primary School*. London: Routledge.

Cox, J. (2005) 'Childhood in crisis: Myth, reality or cause for concern? Perspectives from children, parents and the news media', PhD thesis, Canterbury Christ Church University.

Craft, A. (1994) 'Five and six year-olds' views of friendship', *Education Studies*, 20(2): 181–94.

David, T. (1992) '"Do we have to do this?" The Children Act 1989 and obtaining children's views in early childhood settings', *Children and Society*, 6(3): 204–11.

Denscombe, M. (2007) *The Good Research Guide.* Maidenhead: Open University Press.

Department for Education and Skills (DfES) (2004) *The Children Bill.* London: HMSO.

Department for Children, Schools and Families (DCSF) (2008) *Practice Guidance for the Early Years Foundation Stage.* Nottingham: DCSF.

Dhalberg, G., Moss, P. and Pence, A. (1999) *Beyond Quality in Early Childhood Education and Care: Postmodern Perspectives.* London: Routledge.

Dickins, M. (2004) *Listening as a Way of Life: Listening to Young Disabled Children.* London: National Children's Bureau.

Drummond, M.J. (2002) 'Listening to children talking'. Keynote speech at NCB's Early Childhood Unit's Early Childhood Conference. http://www.ncb.org.uk/dotpdf/open_access_2/edu_lctc_mjdspeech_2002.pdf

Edwards, C., Gandini, L. and Forman, G. (1993) *The Hundred Languages of Children: The Reggio Emilia Approach to Early Childhood Education*, 1st edn. London: Ablex. REGGIO CHILDREN/Centro Internazionale Loris Malaguzzi, Via Bligny,1/a,42124 Reggio Emilia, http://zerosei.comune.re.it/

Edwards, C., Gandini, L. and Forman, G. (1998) *The Hundred Languages of Children: The Reggio Emilia Approach to Early Childhood Education*, 2nd edn. London: Ablex. REGGIO CHILDREN/Centro Internazionale Loris Malaguzzi, Via Bligny,1/a,42124 Reggio Emilia, http://zerosei.comune.re.it/

Epstein, D. (1998) 'Real boys don't work', in D. Epstein, J. Elwood, V. Hey and J. Maw (eds) *Failing Boys? Issues in Gender and Achievement.* Buckingham: Open University Press.

Erwin, P. (1998) *Friendship in Childhood and Adolescence.* London: Routledge.

Folque, M. (2010) 'Interviewing young children', in G. MacNaughton, S. Rolfe and I. Siraj-Blatchford (eds) *Doing Early Childhood Research: International Perspectives on Theory and Practice*, 2nd edn. Buckingham: Open University Press.

Gibbs, S., Mann, G. and Mathers, N. (2002) *Child to Child: A Practical Guide: Empowering Children as Active Citizens.* Available from: http://www.child-to-child.org/guide/index.html

Greig, A. and Taylor, J. (1999) *Doing Research with Children.* London: Sage Publications.

Harcourt, D., Perry B. and Waller, T. (eds) (2011) *Young Children's Perspectives: Ethics, Theory and Research.* Abingdon: RoutledgeFalmer (March 2011, *forthcoming*).

Harvey, R. (2004) 'A toothless watchdog: shortcomings of the mandate for the Children's Commissioner', 2004, cR205, pp. 4–7.

Hawkins, B. (2002) 'Children's drawing, self expression, identity and the imagination', *International Journal of Art and Design*, 21(3): 197–208.

Holliday, A. (2002) *Doing and Writing Qualitative Research*. London: Sage Publications.

Holliday, A. (2007) *Doing and Writing Qualitative Research*. London: Sage Publications.

Hughes, P. (2001) 'Paradigms, methods and knowledge', in G. MacNaughton, S. Rolfe and I. Siraj-Blatchford (eds) *Doing Early Childhood Research: International Perspectives on Theory and Practice*. Buckingham: Open University Press.

Isaacs, S. (1954) *The Educational Value of the Nursery School*. London: British Association for Early Childhood Education.

Jacklin, A. and Lacey, C. (1997) 'Gender integration in the infant classroom: a case study', *British Educational Research Journal*, 23(5): 623–39.

James, A. and Prout, A. (eds) (1997) *Constructing and Reconstructing Childhood*. London: Falmer Press.

Kellett, M. (2010) *Rethinking Children and Research*. London: Continuum.

Kirby, P., Lanyon, C., Cronin, K. and Sinclair, R. (2003) *Building a Culture of Participation: Involving Children and Young People in Policy, Service Planning, Development and Evaluation: A Research Report*. London: Department for Education and Skills.

Kress, G. (1997) *Before Writing: Rethinking the Paths to Literacy*. London: Routledge.

Lancaster, Y. and Broadbent, V. (2010) *Listening to Young Children*, 2nd edn. Maidenhead: Coram Family and Open University Press.

Langsted, O. (1994) 'Looking at quality from the child's perspective', in P. Moss, and A. Pence (eds) *Valuing Quality in Early Childhood Services: New Approaches to Defining Quality*. London: Paul Chapman Publishing.

Langston, A., Abbott, L., Lewis, V. and Kellett, M. (2004) 'Early childhood', in S. Fraser, V. Lewis, S. Ding, M. Kellett and C. Robinson (eds) *Doing Research with Children and Young People*. London: Sage Publications with the Open University.

Lather, P. (1991) *Getting Smart: Feminist Research and Pedagogy with/in the Postmodern*. London: Sage Publications.

Lindon, J. (2003) *Childcare and Early Education: Good Practice to Support Young Children and their Families*. London: Thomson Learning.

Mac an Ghail, M. (1994) *The Making of Men: Masculinities, Sexualities, and Schooling*. Buckingham: Open University Press.

Maccoby, E. (1996) 'Gender as a social category', in W. Bukowski, A. Newcomb and W. Hartup (eds) *The Company they Keep: Friendship in Childhood and Adolescence*. Cambridge: Cambridge University Press.

MacNaughton, G. (2000) *Rethinking Gender in Early Childhood*. London: Paul Chapman Publishing.

Malaguzzi, L. (1996) 'No Way. The Hundred is There', in *The Hundred Languages of Children*. Reggio Emilia: Reggio Children. Centro Internazionale Loris Malaguzzi, Via Bligny, 1/a, 42124 Reggio. Emilia http://zerosei.comune.re.it/

MacNaughton, G. and Hughes, P. (2008) *Doing Action Research in Early Childhood Studies*. Buckingham: Open University Press.

MacNaughton, G., Rolfe, S. and Siraj-Blatchford, I. (eds) (2010) *Doing Early Childhood Research: International Perspectives on Theory and Practice*, 2nd edn. Buckingham: Open University Press.

Mann, G. and Laws, S. (2004) *Involving Children in Research on Violence against Children*. London: Save the Children Fund.

Martin, E. (2005) 'Emotional development and learning in the early years', PhD thesis, Canterbury: Christ Church University.

Mauthner, M. (1997) 'Methodological aspects of collecting data from children: lessons from three research projects', *Children and Society*, 11: 16–28.

Mayall, B. (ed.) (1993) *Children's Childhoods: Observed and Experienced*. London: Falmer Press.

Mayall, B. (2000) 'Conversations with children: working with generational issues', in Christensen, P. and James, A. (eds), *Research with Children: Perspectives and Practices*. London: Routledge.

McNiff, J. (2006) *All you Need to Know about Action Research*. London: Sage Publications.

McNiff, J. and Whitehead, J. (2010) *You and Your Action Research Project*. London: Routledge.

Miles, B. (1994) *Qualitative Data Analysis: An Expanded Sourcebook*. London: Sage Publications.

Millam, R. (2002) *Anti-Discriminatory Practice: A Guide for Workers in Childcare and Education*. London: Continuum.

Morrow, V. and Richards, M. (1996) 'The ethics of social research with children: an overview', *Children and Society*, 10: 90–105.

Mukherji, P. and Albon, D. (2009) *Research Methods in Early Childhood: An Introductory Guide*. London: Sage Publications.

National Children's Bureau (NCB) (2002) 'Including children in social research', *Highlight*, no. 193.

National Children's Bureau (NCB) (2003) *Guidelines for Research*. Available from www.ncb.org.uk/dotpdf/.../research_guidelines_200604.pdf (accessed June 2010).

Oliver, P. (2004) *Writing Your Thesis*. London: Sage Publications.

Pahl, K. (1999) *Transformations: Children's Meaning Making in a Nursery*. Stoke-on-Trent: Trentham Books.

Punch, K. (2009) *Introduction to Research Methods in Education*. London: Sage Publications.

Quortrup, J. (1987) 'Introduction: The sociology of children', *International Journal of Sociology*, 17(3): 3–37.

Roberts-Holmes, G. (2001) 'The whole family: Looking back to jump ahead', *Co-Ordinate, Journal of National Early Years Network*, Spring, issue 80.

Rogoff, B. (2003) *The Cultural Nature of Human Development*. Oxford: Oxford University Press.

Rolfe, S. and Emmett, S. (2010) 'Direct observation', in G. MacNaughton, S. Rolfe, and I. Siraj-Blatchford (eds) *Doing Early Childhood Research: International Perspectives on Theory and Practice*, 2nd edn. Buckingham: Open University Press.

Schön, D. (1987) *Educating the Reflective Practitioner: Toward a New Design for Teaching and Learning in the Professions*. San Francisco, CA: Jossey-Bass.

Sewell, T. (1998) 'Loose canons: Exploding the myth of the "black macho" lad', in D. Epstein, J. Elwood, V. Hey and J. Maw (1998) *Failing Boys? Issues in Gender and Achievement*. Buckingham: Open University Press.

Shields, P. (2009) 'School doesn't feel as much of a partnership': Parents' perceptions of their children's transition from nursery school to Reception class', *Early Years*, 29(3): 237–48.

Siraj-Blatchford, I. and Clarke, P. (2000) *Supporting Identity, Diversity and Language in the Early Years*. Buckingham: Open University Press.

Siraj-Blatchford, J. (2010) 'Surveys and questionnaires: An evaluative case study', in G. MacNaughton, S. Rolfe and I. Siraj-Blatchford (eds) *Doing Early Childhood Research: International Perspectives on Theory and Practice*, 2nd edn. Buckingham: Open University Press.

Skelton, C. (2001) *Schooling the Boys: Masculinities and Primary Education*. Buckingham: Open University Press.

Taylor, A. (2000) 'The UN Convention on the Rights of the Child: Giving children a voice', in A. Lewis and G. Lindsay (eds) *Researching Children's Perspectives*. Buckingham: Open University Press..

Thorne, B. (1993) *Gender Play: Girls and Boys in School*. Buckingham: Open University Press.

United Nations (UN) (1989) *Convention on the Rights of the Child*. New York: United Nations.

Vasconcelos, T. (2008) *'Case study'* in G. MacNaughton and P. Hughes *Doing Action Research in Early Childhood Studies*. Buckingham: Open University Press.

Webster, S. (2002) 'Cinderellas in lonely castles? Perspectives of voluntary preschool supervisors in rural communities', in C. Nutbrown (ed.) *Research*

Studies in Early Childhood Education. Stoke-on-Trent: Trentham Books. pp. 183–98.

West, L. (1996) *Beyond Fragments: Adults, Motivation and Higher Education. A Biographical Analysis.* Basingstoke: Taylor and Francis.

Whitehead, J. (2006) *Action Research: Living Theory.* Sage: London.

Willan, J. (2004) 'Observing children: looking into children's lives', in J. Willan, R. Parker-Rees and J. Savage (eds) *Early Childhood Studies.* Exeter: Learning Matters.

Yap, M.S. (2010) 'Malaysian parents' perspective of pre-school education', unpublished MA dissertation, Institute of Education, University of London.

Yelland, N., Lee, L., O'Rourke, M. and Hanlon, C. (2008) *Rethinking Learning in Early Childhood Education.* Maidenhead: Open University Press.

Yin, R.K. (2009) *Case Study Research: Design and Methods.* London: Sage Publications.

Index

Added to a page number 'f' denotes a figure and 't' denotes a table.